*quick reads to cultivate community & fun activities to* *nection where you live*

# hello
## NEIGHBORS

*Small-Town Living in Big City Suburbs*

GREETINGS. HI. JAMBO. WELCOME. YOO-HOO!
HOW GOES IT? NǏ HĂO. HALLO! BONJOUR.
HI-YA. KUMUSTA. HOLA. S'UP? G'DAY. HELLO.
HEJ. GOOD TO SEE YOU. KON'NICHIWA. YO.
SHALOM. NAMASTE. CIAO. BUENOS DIAS. HOWDY.

### Katie O. Engen

Copyright © 2025 by Katie O. Engen

All rights reserved.

No portion of this book may be reproduced in any form (print or digital, including via shared internet or resource networks) without written permission from the publisher or author, except as permitted by U.S. copyright law.

This publication is designed to provide accurate and authoritative information in regard to the subject matter covered. It is sold with the understanding that neither the author nor the publisher is engaged in rendering legal, investment, accounting or other professional services. While the publisher and author have used their best efforts in preparing this book, they make no representations or warranties with respect to the accuracy or completeness of the contents of this book and specifically disclaim any implied warranties of merchantability or fitness for a particular purpose. No warranty may be created or extended by sales representatives or written sales materials. The advice and strategies contained herein may not be suitable for your situation. You should consult with a professional when appropriate. Neither the publisher nor the author shall be liable for any loss of profit or any other commercial damages, including but not limited to special, incidental, consequential, personal, or other damages.

Cover design by Big Ideas with adapted spot art from Adrien Coquet – Neighbor Icons/Noun Project (CC BY 3.0). Spot illustrations adapted via content license CC BY 3.0.

ISBN 979-8-9867242-9-4

To Good Neighbors
(especially mine)

And to those everywhere who chat in front yards, help happily,
invite fun, notice needs, give when they can, and make time for others -
all with a heart for building strong moments, lives, and communities.

# PREFACE

This book is not fiction. Yet it does offer some pretty idyllic moments that may seem too good to be true. Yet I lived a lot of it. So, the reality is you truly can enjoy well-rounded community life in a suburb that's enmeshed – at times entangled – with a major metropolitan area. Traffic, politics, and resource needs may swamp the headlines. Honest connections (and maybe even a cup of sugar!) between good neighbors can make all the difference.

The opening essay of each chapter comes from a series of Letters to Residents that I wrote as managing editor of a local magazine. The mission then and now is to promote small-scale connection with bright impacts, even in the shadow of big city pressures. I've gently updated the original letters here to create a resource that works cohesively for readers everywhere.

The chapters' essays are followed by ideas to explore and activate the given theme. Savor one chapter per month or read it all at once. Either way, return over time to try the wide range of neighborly options. Nurture your home and community so that in turn, both will better serve you and yours.

Katie O. Engen
Kensington, MD
October 2025

# Contents

1. Introduction — 1
2. The Power of Hello — 3
3. Be Love — 11
4. Is the Music in You? — 19
5. A Total Eclipse of the Sun — 27
6. May Days in Many Ways — 37
7. Dad Power — 45
8. Alaska — 53
9. Summer Daze — 59
10. Second Chances — 67
11. The Taylor Swift Effect — 75
12. Hold the Apostrophe — 83
13. Light It Up — 91
14. Thank You! — 99

## Introduction

# Who Cares What I Think?

Hello, Neighbors!

I've lived in the same house in the suburbs of Washington, DC for about 30 years. I spent most of my younger years only ~10 miles away. Once married, my husband and I moved around the country for about a decade then came back home and raised two girls in the only house we ever bought. Now one daughter is raising our first grandchild with her husband just 20 minutes up the road. Daughter two lives even closer. We truly are locals.

In other words, I know a lot about the sports, shopping, services, social groups, spiritual congregations, synergy, and squeaky wheels of small-town priorities. I've observed, supported, joined, led, and even avoided aspects of this marvelous, sometimes messy, mix of activities with the people who share them.

Despite knowing and loving my hometown, I was not thrilled when the duty of writing the local community magazine's monthly Letter to Residents unexpectedly fell into my lap. I preferred being the behind-the-scenes editor. And didn't think my personal perspective needed any time in the spotlight. Yet the duty had become mine and no way was I going to write one of those masthead letters that just recap a given magazine's monthly content.

Instead, my letters featured the overlapping geography, shared goals, annual cycles, and occasional kerfuffles of local neighborhoods. Soon enough, I began relishing my monthly epistolary opportunity to offer ideas for springboarding awareness, growth, unity, and fun for those who care about community, too.

Most of what I share is 'good old common sense' updated with new resources and tips for extra fun or efficiency. Readers aware of city planning or building trends, may recognize some 'new urbanist' principles here. This was not intentional, yet I embrace the goal for front-porch friendly, interactive new development. I'm happy at least some of my traditional and learn-by-doing ideas overlap with some of today's more formal design principles aimed at creating small-town connections amid or near big cities.

This book is not just a bunch of love letters to small town living. It's a practical guide for folks who want simple and sincere ways to connect with neighbors and friends they haven't yet met. The activities I suggest are scaled for small groups yet can have big impacts. Because really, it's not about what I suggest, but what you do.

Always one for quirky mashups, I bridged themes, resources, age group targets, and activity genres within these chapters. I like to imagine all the successful, satisfying, and likely surprising synergies that will spring from neighbors personalizing and sharing this mix of options.

Like neighbors, these pages are meant to be interactive. Each chapter offers:

- Points to ponder about why connections of all sorts are so important
- Pro tips, practical fun, & a range of prompts on how to foster them

I sincerely hope this book supports your sense of place and inspires readiness to act on behalf of your community.

# THE POWER OF HELLO

Hello, Neighbors!

As a shy pre-teen, I volunteered at a stable with many horses. I'd enter the barn oh-so-quietly, grab a shovel or saddle, and get to work. If the owner was in the barn and realized I had 'forgotten' (again) to offer a greeting, he would track me down in a hot minute, his Hungarian temper already on boil. By this point, my meek-to-embarrassed, "Hi," barely cut it and, boy, did he let me know it.

His delivery may have been off, but my intense mentor was right. There is great power in just saying, "Hello." In a barn full of horses, safety is a factor. But basic manners, respect for elders, and the practice of announcing oneself in a place I dearly wanted to belong all were lessons I value today.

It's not just me. In 2007, the National Institutes of Health published research (PMID: 17624071) about the beneficial power of greeting students at the classroom door. Since then, many related studies have confirmed the impressive positive impacts of greeting individuals personally and consistently. Social connections, self-worth, and standards of achievement all improve thanks to the power of hello. And isn't it delightful that these results hold true across a very wide range of demographics?

Sometimes the chance to say hello isn't as proscribed as a classroom threshold. New places can be uncomfortable or at least unpredictable. Some people shyly avoid eye contact; others boldly greet everyone. While some of the fitting-in phase is personality dependent, anyone likes to feel welcome. How can you help make that happen?

Think about anyone populating your daily routines. Like those you pass in the same grocery aisle every Tuesday evening. Or while out walking the dog at 7 a.m. each day. Have you said hello yet? It's never too late to share a friendly smile or quick greeting. And more interaction is, well...more! Who knows? A bit of commiserating over pasta prices or pet foibles could lead to an Italian potluck or a neighborly pet-sitting partnership. Give it a try – start with, "Hi."

## PONDER & POST

> Hello? Is it me you're looking for?
> Lionel Ritchie

> Hello my friend, hello. So nice to see you out tonight
> Bill Bottrell (perf. by Sheryl Crow)

> Sometimes, just when I say hello in the right way, I'm like, "Whoa, I'm so cool."
> Robert Pattinson

> I don't know why you say goodbye. I say hello.
> The Beatles (Hello, Goodbye)

> When you say, 'hello,' or 'good morning,' you make a connection. And isn't that what being a human is all about?
> Philip Rosenthal

## PRACTICAL | PROACTIVE | PRO-COMMUNITY

### Start Simple & Spread Out

*Meet & Greet*

'Hello' can be shared in a wide variety of ways. Here are a few inspiring examples to try with different groups and ages.

- Masai Jumping, anyone? Go to EnchantedTravels.com and search 'top six **welcome rituals from around the world**' for some very cool greeting ceremonies. (https://tinyurl.com/4pcnm79w)

- Search www.HopefulNeighborhood.org's blog for '15 Ways to **Welcome Your New Neighbors.**'

- ***Sesame Street*** offers *Hola, Gloria!; Hello Song|Brand New Day; Hello, Hello Song* & more on YouTube.

- For more on **the science of greetings**: Allday, R Allan, and Kerri Pakurar. "Effects of teacher greetings on student on-task behavior."*Journal of applied behavior analysis* vol. 40,2 (2007): 317-20. doi:10.1901/jaba.2 007.86-06

- Greet with **sign language**! Visit www.signasl.org/sign/hello or get the ASL app.

- Are you a shy? Adulting while feeling disconnected. Use terms like 'introvert' or 'shyness' as well as the names of your favorite hobbies to find **meetup groups with accommodating options.**

- Search 'hellos-goodbyes' in www.TheWatsonInstitute.org's resources for **adaptive lessons to teach greetings** to those with special needs.

- **Make a 'TED Talk'** about yourself: One funny/funky/finicky trait of mine that people seem to like is [trait]. Here's how I know.

Too complicated? Put on comfy shoes, head out your door, and take a walk. Enjoy the local sites and be sure to say hello to those you meet.

## Go Big & Go Home!

*It's NYE! Greet the New Year & Your Neighbors with a Progressive Party*

This strategy works best with ~8-10 families with kids of a wide variety of ages. Of course, all you DINKS and Super Seniors can join in or follow suit with your crowd.

This is a progressive party, meaning it moves locations intentionally and at set times. So, invite folks within walking distance. It can be your 'same old crew,' but try to include 1-2 households who have yet to get in the mix.

Divide and conquer hosting duties so nobody is working too hard. Plus, the changes keep the party fresh. They also offer easy departure points for youngsters or anyone wanting a graceful exit.

Keep core planning duties to 2-3 organizers but get general buy-in from attendees at least 3 weeks before December 31. The Party Planner(s) will determine the homes to be visited and in what order, set a theme and/or dress code, and coordinate the menu. After details are firm, share clear, concise information with all participating households, preferably by December 27.

Framework & Detail Options:

- Home 1 @ 7:30PM – Get a full group photo! Pick a color and make everything – food, drinks, tableware, balloons, funny hats – match. Most folks will have eaten dinner but offer an array of solid nibbles (color coordinated, of course). Ring a bell or play a song snippet (e.g., *Ease on Down the Road* from *The Wiz*) at ~8:45 as a 10-minute warning to leave and then again to depart just before 9:00. Note: This likely will be the longest stop since people may not arrive until closer to 8. Also, the next hosts should depart at the 'warning bell' or earlier if they have some last-minute set up.

- Home 2 @ ~9:00PM – Game Time! Decorate with pro sport team, trophy, or blue-ribbon themes. Set up classics like Pin the Tail on the Donkey, Twister, Charades, and Corn Hole. Encourage all ages to play together. Create an Adult Zone for Beer Pong or Flip Cup. Provide 'game day' drinks and snacks for all. Ring that 10-minute warning bell and/or play a departing song snippet (e.g., *Ole, Ole, Ole,* the soccer anthem).

- Home 3 @ ~10:15PM – Let's Dance! Disco lights, the street's best sound system, a decades- and genre-spanning playlist, and clear space to move and groove. Sprinkle in some line dances (Macarena, Cotton-Eyed Joe, The Wobble). Set up *Dance, Dance, Revolution*. Get really crazy and have somebody call a Square Dance or demonstrate/lead some Swing Dance. Consider an official Dance Contest or just let the music play. Fuel the fun (and soak up the beverages) with some heftier, but easy to make snacks that keep well like one of those really long subs, a meat & cheese tray/charcuterie board, oven-baked pizza (if it's too late for delivery), and maybe some chips and dips. A fondue station could be fun, too.

- Home 4 @ 11:30PM – All TVs should be set to NYE shows. Scatter noisemakers, hats, and all the celebratory fixings. Offer festive desserts with some fruit and salty nibbles in the mix. By 11:45, set out flutes or cups of champagne and sparkling juice. By ~12:45 ring the departure bell and/or play a final song (e.g., *Closing Time* by Semisonic or *So Long, Farewell* from *The Sound of Music*)

Tips for the Tiniest Celebrants

- Try to have EVERYONE start at Home 1. Be sure to take a group picture! Send those who need it to the house designated as the Kid Krib. Family Teens (and maybe some assisting Tweens) can be the Official Kid Wranglers. Equip the house with snacks, juice boxes, and maybe some late-night pizza. Keep any games simple and toys shareable. Maybe set up 1-2 movies (different rooms, different ages) for later in the party.

- Who needs midnight to have fun? Opt out of late-night anything. Shift the times and menu to enjoy brunch and a Happy <u>Noon</u> Year's Eve. Start at 10:30 a.m., get to House 2 by noon, then shift the party 1-2 more times until ~2:00.

## PROMPTS

### *Wonder – Write – What Next?*

Review the list of greetings above or on the title page.

1. How many can you pronounce? Translate precisely?

2. Which casual greeting suits you best?

3. Which formal one is your favorite?

4. Which ones could you use at work? Or with friends this weekend?

5. Who would be startled, amused, or impressed if you greeted them more formally/casually than usual? Why?

6. Pick a new greeting to try next time you're in a new setting or want to (finally) initiate a connection with a person you see all the time. Why is this the best greeting for you?

List 3 places where you can try your new greeting this week. What response(s) do you predict for each?

1)                     2)                     3)

 Describe or sketch a time you felt the POWER of HELLO as the greeter or greeted.

# BE LOVE

Hello, Neighbors!

Austin Kleon, author of *Steal Like an Artist*, wrote, "Lots of people want to be the noun without doing the verb." He meant that to become proficient and fulfilled, writers must write, dancers dance, nurses nurse, etc. Comedian-actor Stephen Fry or author-dilletante Oscar Wilde may retort Kleon's assertion, claiming a noun locks people into labels, cul-de-sacs, or prescriptive routines. But I lean toward Kleon, adding that to achieve the honor of being a [fill in your aspirational noun of choice here], first do the verb with consistency and passion. Let's consider how this works with the noun/verb interplay of the term, love.

Most Valentines will claim *lover* as their aspirational noun. Ah, romance. Taylor Swift sings in her song, *Lover*, "And there's a dazzling haze, a mysterious way about you, dear. Have I known you 20 seconds or 20 years?" Such a powerful sentiment for those who maintain the dazzle. Of course, romantic love isn't an automatic delight. As depicted in the movie, *Love, Actually*, young Sam's stepfather is relieved to learn Sam's deep sadness is 'nothing worse' than unrequited middle school love. Sam defends his plight by asking with aching woe if there's anything, "Worse than the total agony of being in love?" Yet, after deep commiseration with his stepdad, Sam improves his plight dramatically by taking bold action. Because love is more than a feeling.

Many long-married couples will espouse that lasting love requires action, bold and otherwise. Yes, buy the gift, take the trip, renew the vows! These grand gestures are the cherry on top of many practical ways romantic connections deepen as simple acts accumulate. So, share the chores, playlists, kid carpools, inside jokes, and your most coveted snacks. As Mother Teresa, advised, "Do small things with great love."

Enduring love of any sort is rooted in the term's quietly synonymous phrases that percolate through daily interactions. Phrases like, "Can I get you something to eat?" "I'm glad you're here." "You look cold. Use my scarf." "Text me when you get home." "Stay put. I'll get it." "Here's the signup link to help our neighbors with [insert cause]." Actions nurture kinship. Those platonic, love as a state-of-being connections everyone needs.

Experts say young children interpret happiness, security, and belonging as love. What actions should kids experience – and their grownups prioritize – especially as life's harder realities try to interfere? Being happy comes from making and maintaining healthy choices. Being secure requires learning skills, setting goals, and bouncing back from mistakes. Being welcome comes from participating with others and practicing kindness. So many facets to building, being, and doing love! So many ways to make it happen!

And for the wider community? Reconsider the film, *Love, Actually.* It offers heartwarming, humorous, and hearty advice-by-example for doing and being love that can work for all. As the film ends, the screen fills with a montage of people showing up – with great joy – to greet loved ones at the airport. Hugh Grant as England's prime minister voices, "Whenever I get gloomy with the state of the world, I think about the arrivals gate at Heathrow Airport...It seems to me that love is everywhere. Often, it's not particularly dignified or newsworthy, but it's always there - fathers and sons, mothers and daughters, husbands and wives, boyfriends, girlfriends, old friends... If you look for it, I've got a sneaky feeling you'll find that love actually is all around."

How might your actions help you and others find some of that love which is, indeed, all around?

## PONDER & POST

And now these three remain: faith, hope and love. But the greatest of these is love.
1 Corinthians 13:13, NIV

*Love, love me DO. You know I love you...*
(Hear that emphasis on the action when you sing along?)
Lennon & McCartney

...Agape does not begin by discriminating between worthy and unworthy people, or any qualities people possess. It begins by loving others for their sakes. It is an entirely 'neighbor-regarding concern for others,' which discovers the neighbor in every man it meets. Therefore, Agape makes no distinction between friend and enemy; it is directed toward both. If one loves an individual merely on account of his friendliness, he loves him for the sake of the benefits to be gained from the friendship, rather than for the friend's own sake. Consequently, the best way to assure oneself that love is disinterested is to have love for the enemy-neighbor from whom you can expect no good in return, but only hostility and persecution."
Martin Luther King Jr., 'Stride Toward Freedom: The Montgomery Story'

Friendship is probably the most common form of love.
Stieg Larsson

## PRACTICAL | PROACTIVE | PRO-COMMUNITY

### Start Simple & Spread Out
*How Do I Love Thee?*

- Get Inspired! Search 'love' and your genre of choice @ imdb.com. The goal is to watch one with agape or friendship as the main theme. As you scan the titles & blurbs, notice how many insist love is nothing but agony or romance. Pick a show you've never seen. Enjoy!

- Grab a partner for a few rounds of the hand-clapping game called Concentration 64. Under the general umbrella of *loving actions*, play with categories like, 'actions for Dad/Sibling/Grandparent,' '...for teachers,' for '...new friend,' and more.

- Ever heard of *limerence*? Should it count as a type of love? To decide for yourself, read what AttachmentProject.com offers on love vs. limerence or PsychologyToday.com posts on the 'basics of limerence.' You also can watch 'Uncertainty + Hope = Limerence I The Psychology of 'Unrequited Love' by Adelle Deriquito on YouTube.

### Go Big & Go Home!

*Sometimes Love is Being a Short-Order Cook*

**Super-Quick Quesadillas –** This is toaster oven cuisine at its finest. Snack or dinner, these quesadillas are easy-peasy to personalize for picky palates & varied portions. Also great for novice cooks to practice following a recipe and using an oven.

### Ingredients
(serves 1, tween or bigger)
2 – 10" flour or corn soft tortillas
1/2 cup – fine shredded Mexican-style cheese
[yep, that's it!]

-Line toaster oven pan with foil for easy clean up. Preheat to 425°F.
-Sprinkle cheese on 1/2 of each tortilla. Fold tortillas in half. Stack on the pan.
-Bake until cheese is melted, ~3 minutes. Flipping optional (really!)
-Add a minute for light browning. Add another for crispy edges.

# HELLO, NEIGHBORS! SMALL-TOWN LIVING IN BIG CITY SUBURBS

*It takes longer to read the add-in & prep options than to prepare these packets of golden gooiness. But short-order cooks need options!*

Add-In Options:
spinach leaves (torn to bite-sized), black beans, avocado slices, diced produce (tomato, pepper), diced protein (chicken, shrimp, tofu, fish), salsa, hot sauce, crema
Keep proportions to scale so the tortilla can close.

Prep Options:
- Need more quesadillas? Line up a bunch on a foil-lined cookie sheet in the big oven. Still no flipping needed!
- For 'sophisticated dining,' cook in a cast-iron pan with a bit of butter. Try one flip for even melting and browning.
- List each family member's preferred (or hated) Add-In Options here:




**Snow Day Central** – After everyone tromps inside your house, strips off their snowy garb, and stuffs everything but their boots into your dryer, they need calories asap. If the Super-Quick Quesadillas aren't enough, add these simple & hearty snacks to fuel the next round of Snow Day fun (works on swim days, too).

1. Hot chocolate – Warm milk and chocolate syrup in a big pot. Simmer and stir. Ladle into mugs.
2. Popcorn – Heat veg oil in a large, lidded pot on medium-high heat. Cover the pot's bottom with popcorn kernels. Salt & serve.

Trust me – skip the pre-packaged options. Your nibbling visitors will be excited and impressed by your 'throwback' skills & menu.

## PROMPTS

### *Wonder – Write – What Next?*

What says love more than poetry? Craft a few love poems of your own. See the table for writing prompts and pairings. You can matchmake the formats and genres any way you like.

| Poetry Format | Love Type/Theme |
|---|---|
| HAIKU - 3 lines; syllables per line = 5, 7, 5<br>use careful wording to marry the mystical to the daily<br>(ReadPoetry.com/10-vivid-haikus-to-leave-you-breathless/) | practical action<br>(home or community) |
| COUPLET - 2 lines; AA rhymes<br>use several; mix rhyme patterns e.g., AA-BB-CC-AA<br>(FamilyFriendlyPoems.com/collection/poems-with-couplets) | neighborly niceties |
| SONNET - 15 line in iambic pentameter; rhymes optional<br>use serious to swoon-y theme or tone<br>(PoemAnalysis.com/best-poems/famous-sonnets/) | romantic love |
| LIMERICK - 5 lines; syllables per line = 9,9,6,6,9<br>use AABBA rhyme scheme; can be irreverent<br>(SmartBlogger.com/limerick-examples/) | silly giggles w/friends<br>OR new crush |

Draft & compose here and on the next page. Write your favorite inside a card or letter you'll share with Someone Special.

Take action and spread the love! Share your poems with neighbors, community helpers, in local newsletters, on your socials, and the like.

# Is the Music in You?

H ello, Neighbors!

Even if it's not March when you're reading this, let's consider the month's finer points. First, hooray for more sunlight! Shout out to all the spring break adventurers! And, yes, let's make much ado about St. Patty's Day, Purim, Holi, National Pi (3.14) Day and the rest! Why, with so much fun to be had, it's enough to make you want to break out in song.

But which song should it be? All of us march to the beat of our own drum. In fact, it's the varied tempos, tones, and tracks that orchestrate a community's rhythms. No, we don't always live in perfect harmony, but most everyone agrees that all of God's children have a place in the choir. Speaking of an eclectic choir...

What might be on your Hometown Jams playlist? Think of songs or instrumentals that convey the high notes, tempo, and solo performances of living where you do. It's fine if you're feeling the blues or more hardcore scores since darker notes are important too. To ponder your locally inspired groove, ask yourself...

Are you a former *Uptown Girl* (Billy Joel) loving this quieter scene? Are you usually walking on the *Sunny Side of the Street* (Louis Armstrong) no matter the weather? Love meeting neighbors, shopping, or playing when you're *Out in the Street* (Bruce Springsteen)? Always telling friends, "*Welcome to My House* (Flo Rida) and make yourself at home?" Or do you like a smaller, acapella version of connection like *Won't You Be My Neighbor* (Mr. Rogers)? Are you someone who ponders the days of *Little Pink Houses* (John Mellencamp) or hums *Little Boxes*

(Pete Seeger)? Or would you eagerly do karaoke *Let's Build a House* (Priscilla Renea), *If I Had a Hammer* (Pete Seeger), or *We Built This City* (Starship) with local realtors and builders?

How much of *Mayberry* (Rascal Flatts) can you find on local streets? Do you *Take it Easy* (Eagles) when you're running down the road? Or do you find yourself biting back, *D#*%, This Traffic Jam* (James Taylor), in a minivan packed with young passengers? Sure, there could be some drama in your playlist to reflect what's blowing up in your little circle of *The Suburbs* (Arcade Fire)? But can you focus on what makes it easy to believe there's nothing *More Than My Hometown* (Morgan Wallen)?

Confucious said, "Music produces a kind of pleasure which human nature cannot do without." Hear that? The idea of communities seeking harmonies – literal & figurative - certainly has stood the test of time.

So, c'mon! Drop the beat now and name that tune. Create a playlist that syncopates with your hometown.

## PONDER & POST

Adam Small, a musical artist & mentor, collected quotes by non-musicians (mymusicmasterclass.com). Here are some of the insights he collected from people who think deeply and perhaps more astutely than they can play or sing.

- *"Music gives a soul to the universe, wings to the mind, flight to the imagination, and life to everything.* ~ Plato

- *...I often think in music. I live my daydreams in music. I see my life in terms of music.* ~Albert Einstein

- *Music in the soul can be heard by the universe.* ~Lao Tzu

- *With the truth, all given facts harmonize; but with what is false, the truth soon hits a wrong note.* ~Aristotle

And now from some ladies who ARE the music...

- *Art is about communication. That's why I do it.* ~Dolly Parton

- *Music does a lot of things for a lot of people.* ~Aretha Franklin

- *You're a song written by the hands of God.* ~Shakira

## PRACTICAL | PROACTIVE | PRO-COMMUNITY

### Start Simple & Spread Out
*Do-Re-Mi-Fa-So-La-Ti-Do*

Sing. Whenever, wherever. Just sing. Your live performance in the shower, kitchen, or when walking the dog doesn't have to be amazing, or even in tune, to generate good energy. Need more practical reasons? Some research indicates singing for 10 minutes daily clears sinuses and improves posture.

Sing outside. With earbuds or acapella. Other people may vibe along with you or at least appreciate your moxie - as long as you're cool about the setting. Shy? At least have a song in your heart. Maybe even a personal 'entrance song' or anthem. Relishing that one beloved, on-brand tune will light up your face, put pep in your step, and help you radiate positivity to those you meet. List 3 songs that personify you.

1.

2.

3.

Need more structure? Join a choir. Start a choir. Sing in church (& louder, all you Catholics!).
Need to keep it loose? Make up silly songs for cleaning, house-leaving, or bedtime routines. Yes, even if you don't have young kids.

### Go Big & Go Home!

*Appreciate Songbirds*

cardinals, bluebirds, robins, sparrows, juncos, chickadees, finches, wrens, & more

Hit pause on man-made music to appreciate how songbirds bring the OG, super-native playlists we all need. Literally.

- A healthy songbird population brings robust pollination, insect management, seed dispersal and a beautiful soundtrack to the yards, parks, and woods where you live.

- A songbird is a perching bird (3 toes forward, 1 back) that can produce a wide range of sounds. To sing, birds control muscles surrounding the syrinx, their vocal organ. Every bird has a syrinx at the base of its windpipe, but only songbirds use it tunefully.

- Birdsong is for defending territory and attracting a mate. Even unmelodious songbirds (looking at you, crows) sing for these reasons.

- Most songbird hatchlings have few songs. The young must listen to and imitate parents to expand their playlists. Innovators that add a note or change a rhythm often grow to be the most attractive mates.

*Save the Songbirds*
populations are declining, mostly for easily preventable reasons.

1. Keep cats contained. Free-roaming owned cats and feral cats together kill ~2.4 BILLION songbirds each year. Yikes.

2. Mother Nature knows best. Plant native plants or even wildscape your yard to provide safe food and good shelter.

3. In February natural food and unfrozen water can be scarce. Provide both. Trim plants and bushes in fall or winter to avoid disturbing springtime nest making, eggs, hatchlings, and fledglings.

4. Clean up routinely. Dirty feeders launch or spread disease. Fallen seed attracts rats and racoons who will predate nests. Hawks hunt where songbirds gather regularly, so limit drama at feeders and water stations by using them only for harsh seasonal conditions.

5. Window collisions kill ~1 BILLION songbirds yearly, so make windows visible to birds. Close curtains or blinds at least halfway. Add a stencil or decals that are at least 4-inches wide with gaps in the design that are no bigger than 2-inches wide.

6. Light pollution disturbs local nesting and feeding patterns as well as seasonal migrations. Do not keep outside lights on all night. Use timers. Aim necessary beams low. Use lower wattage and/or red bulbs. Learn more @ DarkSky.org.

7. Is your coffee habit 'for the birds?' Search 'bird friendly coffee' @ nationalzoo.si.edu to find new brews. Small sips add up!

8. Learn more @ NativeSongbirdCare.org; search 'help songbirds.' They give phone advice on helping sick or injured birds, too. Join other Citizen Scientists @ www.NationalBirdFeedingMonth.com or @ www.BirdCount.org to support and track bird populations.

You can save figurative songbirds, too! First, don't download songs for 'free.' Learn how to protect human music creators' rights @ unison.audio/performi ng-rights-organizations. Join the choir of helpers like the American Society for Composers, Authors, & Publishers (ascap.com), Broadcast Music, Inc. (BMI.org), or SESAC Performing Rights (seasac.org).

## PROMPTS

### *Wonder – Write – What Next?*

HEY, MR. DJ – Create two playlists. One to represent your <u>household's</u> rhythms and rhymes. A second that captures the tones, genres, and beats of your <u>neighborhood</u> or team, extended family, book club, etc.). Aim for ~10 songs per list. All one genre is fine, but so is a funky mix.

- Post your Household Jams list on the fridge and ask any other DJs in the house for feedback. They can create their own, too.

- Play your Hometown Jams list at the next community event (street gathering, fire station open house, BBQ). Post the playlist on the neighborhood listserv or similar and invite input. How many different generations (by age or tenure in neighborhood) can you get involved?

NOTE-WORTHY THOUGHTS – Jot down your responses to these additional quotes gleaned by Adam Small & the related prompts:

Can music really soothe the savage beast?

*If one should desire to know whether a kingdom is well governed, if its morals are good or bad, the quality of its music will furnish the answer. ~Confucious*
Is the impact of your government (local or otherwise) or group organization more like discordant jazz or well-blended harmony? Think of one action you can take to orchestrate or sustain positive notes.

*Music is the universal language of mankind."* ~Henry Wadsworth Longfellow
*Music is what tells us that the human race is greater than we realize.* ~Napoleon Bonaparte
Do you agree with either? Which piece of music, body of work, or musical genre supports or refutes your opinion?

*Music is the language of the spirit. It opens the secret of life bringing peace, abolishing strife.* ~Kahlil Gibran
Are music festival fundraisers established by the likes of the Concert for Bangladesh, Band Aid, USA for Africa as well as those focused on cultural exchange like globalFEST still relevant to bringing peace and abolishing strife? How and why?

Can music at least settle a few household squabbles or fretting neighbors? Experiment and see!

*Where words fail, music speaks.* ~Hans Christian Andersen
*Music is the shorthand of emotion.* ~Leo Tolstoy
Can't get your kids to clean up? Stop the word wars. Lighten the tone with that old Barney *Clean Up* song. Arguing with an angry teen? Share a headbanger to vent frustrations together, then ask the teen for a song that helps convey the core of what's wrong. In a snit with your long-term-lover? Try humor like *50 Ways to Leave Your Lover* (Paul Simon) or *We Are Never Getting Back Together* (Taylor Swift). Or go super-romantic by playing the song from your first date or wedding. Need more drama? Try the soundtrack from *Moulin Rouge*, a Disney classic, or *Love and Basketball*.

*You couldn't not like someone who liked the guitar."* ~Stephen King, 'The Stand'
Invite some experts to set a cool vibe. Eric Clapton, Stevie Ray Vaughn, Joni Mitchell, Slash, B.B. King, Santana, H.E.R., & so many more. Play a track. Heck, play air guitar, too! Enjoying riffs together can only help ease tension, make a new friend, or just get silly with your household or neighborhood band.

# A Total Eclipse of the Sun

Hello, Neighbors!

What were you doing during the Path of Totality in April 2024? Were you within or adjacent that dark corridor? Did you eagerly don funny glasses and stare skyward for a glimpse of a full solar eclipse? Did you join the many *ooh*-ing and *aah*-ing over its coveted 'Diamond ring effect' corona? Just over the moon with excitement?

I was not and did not. I'd hoped to get swept up in an amazing space science event. But mostly I was distracted by how space opera-y 'Path of Totality' sounded. Especially when exclaimed by zealous commentators and super fans.

Nonetheless, while far from the Path of Totality, at zero hour I decided to see what I could see. I didn't have proper glasses, so I tracked the eclipse via NASA online and sat on my deck awaiting the birds and bugs to fall silent under a midday, pseudo-medieval shadow.

It was interesting. And I appreciated others' excitement. But the truth is, while I love *Star Trek*'s unifying themes and the Enterprise's mission *to explore strange new worlds; to seek out new life and new civilizations; to boldly go where no man has gone before*, the lure of "Beam me up, Scotty!" is just not for me.

I prefer to explore astronomical awesomeness that hits a bit closer to home. Especially in the warmer months. Things like tracking long shadows with a toddler. Seeking shady lanes on hot training runs. Reveling in the coolness of a moonlit seascape. Yes, the solar cycles writ large are doing awesome things. But I'm down here just seeking 'flip-flops on the ground' harbingers of summertime.

In 2025, the Northern Hemisphere's Summer Solstice was Friday, June 20, 2025, at 10:42 PM EDT (2:42 AM UTC on June 21). Why it's time of day differs roughly six hours from the Summer Solstice of 2024 (Thursday, June 20, at 4:51PM EDT) is a probably a space science situation of literally galactic proportions. One that I should be eager to unravel. But my mind really only cares that on the Summer Solstice we get the longest daylight hours of the year. Sorry, sleep lovers, it's also the shortest night.

Here are more facts to ground the Summer Solstice for any others sharing my Earth-bound perspective. The word 'solstice' comes from *sol* (sun) and *sistere* (to stand still), both Latin. As etymology goes, it's pretty literal. On June 20th, the Sun appears to stop its daily advance northward to then begin its reverse journey on the 21st. For most folks that means the Sun rises very far to the left on the horizon (its farthest, actually) and sets way over to the right (its most distant spot). Also, this is when the North Pole is at its maximum tilt (about 23.5 degrees) toward the Sun. Meaning, the Northern Hemisphere receives sunlight at the most direct angle of the year.

I'll take that angle. Because for me June 20th means warm light is beaming into my home in places usually lacking a direct sunbath. And solar noon (don't confuse it with clock-time noon), will be a highlight for me. Because I'll be chasing shadows with any available toddler and laughing about how our Peter Pan tag-alongs are the shortest they will be all year.

Whether you tether aspects of outer space to local gravity or strive to launch into infinity and beyond, try to look on the sunny side of the social connections, scholarship, and silliness that find your orbit.

## PONDER & POST

Twinkle Twinkle, Little Star. How I wonder what you are. Up above the world so high. Like a diamond in the sky.
                                                      Jane Taylor

Remember to look up at the stars and not down at your feet. Try to make sense of what you see and wonder about what makes the universe exist. Be curious.
                                        Stephen Hawking

Earth is a small town with many neighborhoods in a very big universe.
                                                     Ron Garan

To understand ourselves, others, and the world around us, we need to be able to change and adapt our perspectives.
                                      Albert Einstein

Life is about perspective...ultimately you have to zoom out.
                                      Whitney Wolfe Herd

You will find that many of the truths we cling to depend greatly on our own point of view.
                              Obi-Wan Kenobi, 'Return of the Jedi'

## **PRACTICAL | PROACTIVE | PRO-COMMUNITY**

### Start Simple & Spread Out
*What is a Solar Eclipse?*

Help young scientists explore eclipses with these learning stars:

- Wiggle and Giggle-*Moon and Stars Lullaby for Babies | Soothing Voice & Relaxing Sleep Music* $20^+$min., nap & quiet time

- NASA Space Place-*What Is a Solar Eclipse?* simple graphics, ~2min., PreK&up

- Scholastic-*What You Need to Know About Solar Eclipses | STEM Video for Kids* realistic images, ~3min., Age 8&up

- Science.NASA.gov offers *The April 8 Total Solar Eclipse: Through the Eyes of NASA*, 5-min read with video clips, 12&up

- GreatAmericanEclipse.com offers adult-friendly recaps and glimpses ahead of eclipses worldwide.

- Be a Trekkie. Find out today's or any day's StarDate at 03.

- CalculatorAcademy.com/stardate-calculator.

*What Else is Out There?*

Picture books can tickle both the brain and funny bone.
1 *Space Block* by Christopher Franceschelli
2 *Astronaut in Training* by Aneta Cruz
3 *Life on Mars* by Jon Agee
4 *Touch the Brightest Star* by Christie Matheson
5 *Faces of the Moon* by Bob Crelin
6 *The Sun Is Kind of a Big Deal* by Nick Seluk
7 *Twinkle Twinkle, Little Star – I Know Exactly What You Are* by Julia Kregenow
8 *Pluto Gets the Call* by Adam Rex
9 *The Darkest Dark* by Chris Hadfield
10 *Nature's Light Spectacular: 12 stunning scenes of Earth's greatest light shows* by Katy Flint

*Starry, Starry Sidewalk*

Design a solar (system)-powered, outdoor mosaic. Enjoyable for all ages.

1. Gather colored chalk, painter's or masking tape, and some galactically fun facts from the resources above.

2. Pick a spot on your sidewalk (or similar) removed from traffic and other busy-ness so you can be safe while creating. Bonus points if passers-by can enjoy the finished art.

3. Start small to test your timeline and tolerance levels. Focus on one sidewalk 'panel' or similarly distinct coverage area then expand when ready.

4. Imagine a design to fill the space. Think 'stained glass windows' more than complicated organic figures or layered sketches.

5. Tape off simple shapes – lines, angles, rectangles, triangles, or block letters - to fill the allotted space. Tape off a boarder, too. Need curves? Form them by using small pieces of tape.

6. Color the full area. Take your time. Handwrite or tape out & color letters to label or a caption the art.

7. Step carefully as you remove the tape. *Et voilà!*

### Go Big & Go Home!

*Beam Bright to Cast Long Shadows*

As Earth spun, the 2024 Path of Totality entered the US from Mexico into Texas then traveled through Oklahoma, Arkansas, Missouri, Illinois, Kentucky, Indiana, Ohio, Pennsylvania, New York, Vermont, New Hampshire, and Maine before heading to the North Atlantic. Though it was a path of darkness, it inspired a lot of shiny excitement, warm gatherings, and bright thinking. All in very specific hometown locations. How brilliant!

What kind of happy shadows can you cast across you path?

- Know anyone who lives in the states listed above? Maybe even someone whose orbit you've fallen out of? Send a letter, postcard, email, text, or social media message just to say hello. The universe is vast, so be a point of light for someone today.

- Join one of NASA's Citizen Science projects @ science.NASA.gov/citizen-science to help collect data about space.

- Donate to science teachers in schools near you or in one of the states listed above. Search TeacherLists.com or contact the state's science education organization. Maybe take a wider view, too, by supporting the International Planetarium Society.

- Plan a solar eclipse escapade! See the 'Future Eclipses' option under the Totality tab @GreatAmericanEclipse.com for where and when to go. Make it a destination vacation for extended family or friends.

- Star-crossed lovers and starry-night romantics alike can 'buy' a star in someone's name via various commercial agents. Just know that the International Astronomical Union's process is the only official way stars receive science-accepted names.

## PROMPTS

### *Wonder – Write – What Next?*

Consider the quotes in the PONDER & POST section and annotate the list. Which ones align with my tendency to eschew (or at least remain rather unexcited about) deep space stuff? Which quotes clash with my approach to space appreciation?

Why do you think I chose to share each quote with you? Which do you like best and why? Jot your thoughts here:

 Find a new quote or lyric that fits my Earth-bound (but upbeat!) mindset shared in the opening essay. Note your quote here:

*Large Scale Notes*

On June 3, 2025, the European Space Agency (ESA) turned 50 on the 200th birthday of Austrian 'Waltz King' Johann Strauss II. ESA celebrated by blasting a live performance of Strauss's famous *The Blue Danube Waltz* into space. The performance also was livestreamed in New York City, Madrid, and Vienna. It accompanied a radio transmission into space of the same number which was prerecorded to avoid technical issues in converting sound files to radio waves. This musical mission echoes NASA's 50th anniversary celebration in 2008 when they sent The Beatles *Across the Universe* into space.

Do you prefer ESA's or NASA's selection? Why is one better for greeting the universe?

List 5+ songs for your 'Hello, Out There!' playlist. Use a variety of genres and musical eras.

1
2
3
4
5

*Your Constellation*

Draw and name a constellation, including lines to connect the stars, that represents your or your household's role within your small-town neighborhood. Sketch the wider galaxy of your metro area surrounding your personalized constellation. What other constellations pop up, too?

# May Days in Many Ways

Hello, Neighbors!

Hooray for the merry, merry month of May! There's so much to celebrate among the many adjacent-to-overlapping cultures we share. With little effort you can find something to appreciate, support, or memorialize on every day of the month (e.g. see nationalday365.com). There are the traditional or particularly popular dates that most everyone knows like May Day (1$^{st}$), Star Wars Day (May the 4$^{th}$ be with you), Cinco de Mayo (duh!), Mother's Day (2$^{nd}$ Sunday), and Memorial Day (last Monday). Not to mention the many quirky days for small-but-mighty entities like birds, chocolate chips, rescue dogs, wine, and sunscreen.

Many of us also are rooted to key events like Vesak or Buddha Day (dates vary by country), the National Day of Prayer (1$^{st}$ Thursday), or Shavout (7 weeks after Passover). Then there are the month-long dedications that recognize groups and causes including Asian American & Pacific Islander Heritage, Mental Health Awareness, Jewish American Heritage, National Clean Air, No Mow May (save the baby pollinators), and many more.

So many choices! So much to honor and enjoy! But hold on a sec. Your month should not become May-hem or a May Daze. Don't force the fun. Don't let the unique become inane. And don't cram calendars or shopping carts for an endless stream of overstimulating 'command performances.' In the process of pursuing small parties or pomp & circumstances at home, with others, or in new niches, don't undermine your peace.

Right about now the existentialists, the yin & yang-ers in our midst, might be pondering another use of the term May Day. It is, after all, a distress signal, a cry for help. And it's true that while many celebrate, others face struggles ranging from unfunny bloopers, to mounting difficulties, to acute or prolonged trauma. How does one balance or sustain joy given the existence of grave counterpoints? Here's what some well-respected yet humble thinkers suggest:

Jennifer Dukes Lee, a former headline news journalist, offered, "When we neglect to celebrate, we deepen the wound of the world."

The author of Ecclesiastes wrote, "For every thing there is a season, and a time to every purpose under Heaven (3:1-2, ASV)," and Paul wrote in Romans (12:15, NIV), "Rejoice with those who rejoice; mourn with those who mourn."

Dalai Lama & Archbishop Desmond Tutu shared in *The Book of Joy*, "Discovering more joy does not...save us from the inevitability of hardships and heartbreaks. In fact, we may cry more easily, but we will laugh more easily, too. Perhaps we are just more alive. Yet as we discover more joy, we can face suffering in a way that ennobles rather than embitters. We have hardship without becoming hard. We have heartbreak without being broken."

Mother Theresa said, "Joy is a net of love by which you can catch souls." Suggesting that perhaps, in turn, you can help them.

Choosing to celebrate is not being tone-deaf to its opposite.

We live in a time and place where we are free to celebrate in a myriad of ways that enrich our community. So, yes, plan for poignant, purposeful observations of our national holidays and annual highlights. Make time for silly traditions, too. Seek both the big, bold, bright differences and the more diminutive or diverse details of celebration. Mostly, embrace how unifying it can be when members of a community seek joy along intertwining paths.

Make it Merry <u>&</u> Meaningful, Neighbors!

## PONDER & POST

*Celebrate This*

Darkness cannot drive out darkness; only light can do that.
Martin Luther King, Jr.

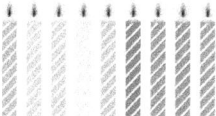

Joy does not simply happen to us. We have to choose joy and keep choosing it every day.
Henri J.M. Nouwen

Celebration has many different outfits, but she always wears the same beautiful dancing shoes.
Mary Anne Radmacher

## PRACTICAL | PROACTIVE | PRO-COMMUNITY

### Start Simple & Spread Out
*Welcome to My House*

"Open up the champagne, pop!
It's my house, come on, turn it up, uh
Hear a knock on the door and the night begins
'Cause we done this before, so you come on in
Make yourself at my home, tell me where you been
Pour yourself something cold, baby, cheers to this
Sometimes you gotta stay in
And you know where I live
Yeah, you know what we is
Sometimes you gotta stay in, in
Welcome to my house
Baby, take control now
We can't even slow down
We don't have to go out
Welcome to my house
Play that music too loud
Show me what you do now
We don't have to go out..."

Flo Rida
(lyrics by Ross Golan, Johan Carlsson, Marco Borrero, Roy Hammond, Tramar Dillard)

Be like Flo Rida. Celebrate hospitality, freedom, and comfort. Any day of the week.
What kind of Gathering-for-No-Reason could you host for tonight? Jot 3 quick ideas here. Then, large or tiny – do it!

## Go Big & Go Home!

### *Take Care of the Bugs*

(Mosquitoes Are for the Birds)

Try this kid-friendly, biodiversity-enhancing way to share your outdoor space with family and neighbors – not swarms of mosquitoes. Set it up early each spring to impede mosquito population explosion as the weather warms.

Avoid fogging and spraying via commercial services or DIY products because covering your yard with pesticides is literally overkill. Most common abatement options will harm bees, butterflies, fireflies, frogs, beneficial bugs, and nesting birds. These chemicals are not especially efficient, either. Fog dissipates before getting only a small percentage of adult mosquitoes. And it does not keep mosquitoes from breeding or laying larvae for another generation.

Native plants and other garden standards need pollinators to thrive, yet mosquito fogging kills those helpful insects, too. Many native birds expend incredible energy all spring and summer. They need mosquitoes and other pesticide-susceptible critters in their diets to stay healthy

No, you don't have to abandon your yard or get bitten all summer. Instead, "Stop the bite. Save the buzz," by trying the Mosquito Bucket Challenge (see FB, Insta, or YouTube). As the creators at Homegrown National Park explain, "The Mosquito Bucket Challenge is a simple way to protect pollinators, birds, frogs, fireflies, and your family—without toxic sprays. By safely targeting mosquito larvae, each bucket helps save the wildlife that fogging puts at risk. It's safe, it's affordable, it's better for biodiversity. And it actually works."

Buckets parlay the mosquitoes' habit of laying eggs in standing water. Challenge participants fill a 'bucket of doom' with 'mosquito tea' to interrupt the mosquito life cycle before any get airborne. All while leaving other pollinators, pesticide-endangered critters, pets, and people alone. Each Mosquito Bucket contains *Bacillus thuringiensis israelensis* or Bti, a natural soil bacterium found in commercially available mosquito dunks. Bti kills the larvae before they grow, fly, and bite.

## The Mosquito Bucket Challenge

1. Get a 5-gallon bucket or similarly sized container. Restaurants, bakeries, and grocers discard buckets from icing, oil, etc. Ask! Keep that freebie out of a landfill.

2. Using permanent markers or paint pens, decorate the bucket with bright flora, fauna, and 'Save the Birds' or 'Save the Fireflies' messages. Or use a color/design to camouflage the bucket.

3. Add water until the bucket is 2/3 full. Drill a hole in the bucket's side just above this level so captured rainfall drains out.

4. Make 'mosquito tea.' Add a small handful of dead leaves or grass clippings. Leave a lot of surface area on the water for mosquitoes to land and lay eggs. 'Funky' water attracts mosquitoes. Leave the bucket in the sun for ~2 days to expedite funkiness.

5. Break your dunk with Bti and add ~1/4 of it tothe water. Many brands are available at hardware stores, agricultural outlets, and garden centers.

6. Cover the bucket with its own lid - securely. Drill ~10 quarter-sized holes into the lid to allow mosquitoes to enter. No lid? Use a piece of wide-holed mesh and secure it tightly with zip ties to cover the bucket. The aim is to keep bigger critters and/or kids out.

7. Place the bucket in a quiet, shady area, away from your house, play areas, or hangout spots. Set it out of reach (i.e., high or behind a gate) from pets or kids.

8. Add more water as needed from evaporation. Use more buckets for a larger yard.

9. Spread the word! Show neighbors. Post pics. Invite others to the #MosquitoBucketChallenge.

## PROMPTS

### *Wonder – Write – What Next?*

#### *A Timely Tweet*

Create yard art or digital images to share via socials by recreating this sample message.

Find a photo or draw an image (on your own signs or a mosquito bucket) of the Acadian Flycatcher. Include/adapt this text:

> I'm the Acadian Flycatcher (Empidonax virescens). I live in the woods along streams and creeks. I winter in northern Central America. I summer here and raise my young. I eat flying insects like mosquitoes, Mayfly, and moths. Commercial sprays and fogging kill my food. My nesting population has declined in this area. Please help!

Create a whole flock of art using birds or other critters you discover in your own yard. This also works nicely in public gardens, especially libraries and schools (with permission).

#### *A Time Capsule Letter*

Pick your favorite quote from any in the main essay or Ponder & Post section above. Use it to inspire a letter you write to be opened sometime in the future – 1 year, 1 decade – you decide. The letter can be to yourself, a child, or a friend.

1. Include the quote. Then put it in your own words. Or distill it into a poem or simple, repeatable mantra. A mix of sincerity and silly is fine. Doodles welcome, too.

2. Set a goal for how you will remind yourself of the quote's importance to you. And/or how you will try to bring its essence into the intended recipient's life. Include this as a specific, measurable goal in the letter for reference later.

3. Store the letter in a safe place. Mark your (digital) calendar with reminders to enact your goal and/or to open and read the letter.

Jot notes for or directly draft your letter here. Transfer the final version to a card or stationery to save carefully.

# DAD POWER

Hello, Neighbors!

Let's celebrate fathers and father-figures.

Some of you may recall the beer commercial featuring a father and son who are competitive-but-close, especially when it comes to their busy, international racing careers. Harry Chapin's song, *Cats in the Cradle* plays along to tug at heartstrings. When Chapin croons, "You know we'll have a good time then, Dad…" the commercial audience is supposed to be touched by the abiding closeness of father and son. Of course, anyone who knows that song's full lyrics realizes it's about a lifetime of surface-level touch points and missed opportunities.

By contrast, I've known many great dads, starting with my own and raising kids with another. We live in a thriving community with plenty of OG and newbie dads all striving to make it work. But what exactly is the 'it' that must work? Connection. Consistent, dedicated connection. All those moments – from tiny to milestone – that fathers and father figures share with their kids also have exponential impacts. Because pouring into the household also means enhancing the critical foundation of healthy communities.

I collected input from some this-generation dads who are all-in on nurturing kids in ways to help the household, build neighborhoods, and impact wider communities. Some of these young dads are first-timers, others are busily parenting their second or third edition. All of them are daddy-ing as if they don't want to miss anything – from dirty diapers to first dances – along the way. Here are some of their freshly realized insights threaded with inputs they're recycling from the OGs in their life.

How to Dad Like You Mean It

1. Look for dads with kids a few months or even several years older than yours. Kids that are engaged with whatever setting they're in, well-mannered, and clearly happy to be with dad. Or at least respecting what he's offering. Then watch and learn. What you notice working should sync well with current resources and realities (e.g., managing digital devices). But don't overlook modern twists on classic techniques (redirecting vs. demanding).

2. Even the hard stuff is easier than you think because love + patience + humor can smooth over any skill deficits and insecurities. Also, fake it until you make it. When in doubt, ask others for insights.

3. Dive into the daily caregiving and housekeeping like you own it – because you do. More bluntly, don't act like a babysitter or hired housekeeper who needs direction at every bleat from the baby or overflowing laundry basket.

4. Plan ahead. In detail. And follow through. Plan A, the established routines, can make for a chill babyhood & beyond. Plans B-Z will get you through the children's meltdowns and mishaps – and yours.

5. It's okay to rough house – but follow the cues. Different kids will signal or say different things when it's time for the bigger person to stop. Respond accordingly and reinforce listening amid the pack if you have one. Boys and girls of all ages need to recognize and respect limits.

6. Laugh. Kids are goofy, loud, sweet, and exhausting. Sometimes all at once. Humor helps. Yes, even Dad Jokes.

Sure, there's some universality to this list of advice. But let's face it, dads do it their way. And thank goodness. Here's to the dads and father figures, be they biological, adoptive, step, stand-in, deployed, or distanced from their babies (of any age), who are making it their business to raise our next generation of great kids and good neighbors.

If you're reading this in June, well...Happy Father's Day! And of course, all this wisdom applies the other 11 months of the year. After all, a dad's importance, his work, and his love are never-ending.

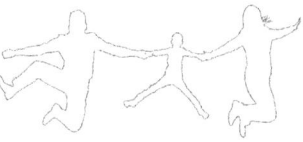

## PONDER & POST

A good father is one of the most unsung, unpraised, unnoticed, and yet one of the most valuable assets in our society.
Billy Graham

The nature of impending fatherhood is that you are doing something that you're unqualified to do, and then you become qualified while doing it.
John Green

Fathering is a difficult and perilous journey and is done well with the help of other men.
John L. Hart

One of the greatest things a father can do for his children is to love their mother.
Howard W. Hunter

> It is easier to build strong children than to repair broken men.
> — Frederick Douglass

> Being a great father is like shaving. No matter how good you shaved today, you have to do it again tomorrow.
> — Reed Markham

> Like so much between fathers and sons, playing catch was tender and tense at the same time.
> — Donald Hall

> Children need models rather than critics.
> — Joseph Joubert

> When you teach your son, you teach your son's son.
> — The Talmud

## PRACTICAL | PROACTIVE | PRO-COMMUNITY

### Start Simple & Spread Out
*Dad-Friendly Resources*

These programs offer inspiring and individualizable insights to quality fathering. If joining one of these options doesn't work for geographical or other reasons, consider how best to adapt the mission, milestones, or mantra of a program for use in your household or community.

**Father Movement, Inc.** (www.fatherm.org) – "Dads are essential to a child's well-being. To improve the lives of our future generations we support fathers to be positively, physically, and emotionally engaged in the lives of their children." **Key Words: Daddy Olympics, health & nutrition, lasting relationships**

**Dads Group** (www.dadsgroup.org) – "We focus on the early years; the impacts last a lifetime. We promote positive parenting for fathers and father figures and give new Dads the support and connection they need." **Key Words: father-friendly, social relationships, Dads at Work, Man with a Pram, research-based**

**Postpartum Support International** (www.postpartum.net; type 'dad' in search bar) – "You are not alone. One in ten dads experiences postpartum depression and 5-15% develop an anxiety disorder at some point during the pregnancy or the first year postpartum." **Key Words: help for dads, connections, resources, answers**

**National Fatherhood Initiative®** (www.fatherhood.org) – "One in four children grow up without a biological, step, or adoptive father. We partner with communities and organizations to unlock the transformative power of involved fatherhood. We fuel your family-strengthening efforts with proven solutions." **Key Words: father inclusion, strong families, training with impact**

**National At-Home Dad Network** (https://athomedad.org) – "Finding a group of local dads is one of the most vital parts of having a successful, enriching, and less stressful time as an at-home dad. The community, support, and camaraderie encourage at-home dads to join each other." **Key Words: group listings by state, online, start-your-own**

**Parents Helping Parents** (www.parentshelpingparents.org/fathers-support-group) – "Kids need dads, too. Connect with other dads and discover effective strategies for navigating fatherhood." **Key Words: trained facilitators, never dad bashing, Zoom meetings**

**Fathering Together** (https://fatheringtogether.org/fatherhood-support-groups) – "We seek to transform dads into positive change agents through communities of support and accountability which provide space for vulnerability and work toward equitable practices." **Key Words: proactive & practical skills, dads in community**

The Father's Rights Movement (https://tfrm.org) – "We are men and women committed to helping loving fathers enjoy their full rights and responsibilities, as well as helping children have their fathers in their lives. Research suggests that equal, shared parenting is most beneficial for the children." **Key Words: equal shared parenting advocacy**

Even if you or those you know in a fathering role do not need a mentoring hand right now, it's heartwarming and eye-opening to discover and explore such important, clever supports for building strong fathers in all walks of life.

### Go Big & Go Home!

*Everybody's Gotta Eat*

Be the Weekly Waffles Dad! Everyone loves to gather for hot breakfasts – or dinners that feature breakfast food. Either way, it's a delicious reason to gather. Prep some sliced fruit or berries and maybe bacon in tandem with cooking the waffles. Ask the kids to help!

### Dad's Weekly Waffles

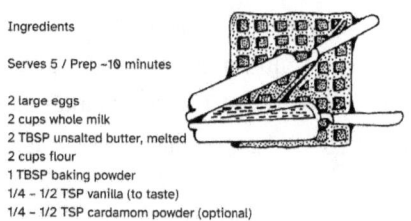

Ingredients

Serves 5 / Prep ~10 minutes

2 large eggs
2 cups whole milk
2 TBSP unsalted butter, melted
2 cups flour
1 TBSP baking powder
1/4 – 1/2 TSP vanilla (to taste)
1/4 – 1/2 TSP cardamom powder (optional)

1. Preheat waffle iron to medium high.

2. Whisk together the eggs, milk, melted butter, and vanilla (optional) in a large bowl.

3. Whisk into the same bowl the flour, baking powder, and cardamom powder until it all combines.

4. Scoop one ladle of batter onto the waffle iron. Using the iron's timer or light sensor, cook until lightly browned.

5. Serve with butter, syrup, and/or berries. On special days, break out the whipped cream.

If this recipe seems too much, just add the dash of cardamom and/or vanilla to a box mix and call it a win. Heck, even toasting frozen waffles and adding great toppings is yummy. Fancy or funky, just do your thing consistently each week.

Once your waffle routine is easy-peasy, consider inviting a few neighbors or hosting a street party for brunch. Make it a fundraiser for trees on your street or equipment for a nearby park.

After you've hosted guests a few times, consider scaling up to host a monthly or annual event for the wider community. Expand your fundraising goals with 'suggested donations' from diners that can cover costs and allow some proceeds to donate.

Local churches and other community groups may have space for prep and hosting plus some volunteers to help. Kiwanis, a national pro-community organization with deeply rooted local chapters, offers these well-vetted tips for hosting public-facing events: https://www.kiwanis.org/tips-for-hosting-a-successful-pancake-breakfast.

## PROMPTS

### *Wonder – Write – What Next?*

Write up to 3 DAD GOALS for weekly use. These are not Big Mission Statements, but measurable, attainable, and hopefully fun! Examples:

- We will share one picture book or book chapter at least three nights per week. [all ages; Zoom or record if distance is a factor]

- I will write one silly or supportive note or text 'for no real reason' to my kid(s). Bonus for notes left in 'surprising' spots.

- We will tackle [name of chore] together each week.

Create goals for the YEAR and the DECADE, too.

### My Weekly TO DAD List

1.

2.

3.

### Dad-in-the-'Hood Goals to Aim for This Year
[Consider some goals for building community or networks, too.]

1.

2.

3.

### My DAD-spirations to Achieve within 10 Years
[travel? training? total immersion? trust-building?]

1.

2.

3.

# ALASKA

Hello, Neighbors!

Before leaving for our trip to Alaska one recent July, the idea of visiting snow-capped mountains, rainy forests, and icy waters just as summer was finally arriving in my hometown left me a bit, well...cold. I was wrong. It was worth it.

The sparkling white glaciers laced with denser blue ice were stunning. One named Margerie calved as our ferry idled nearby. And Ferris's dark, debris-packed face offered us brutal beauty. Distant glaciers were jewels peering down from surrounding peaks. It was awesome being amid these massive frozen tributaries that still recede and advance in the immense bay carved by the Grand Pacific Glacier. Beneath pristine skies, the land seems both fresh and ancient. Tlingit clan history was writ large. Their Homeland ties changed forever by the 'Little' Ice Age, yet their fortitude alongside National Park Service collaborations shows that timeless tribal goals are still in action with new impacts today.

Hiking miles in a rainforest downpour was a joy as stony heights, waterfalls, and animal sightings beckoned. Up close, the path, rocks, logs, and Sitka spruce branches were blanketed by lush, 'over-sized' – to my East Coast eyes - moss, fungus, and lichen. Stretches of mud, ice, and rocks meant slowing down or turning back, which revealed new perspectives. Constantly rushing streams and watery cascades layered in a lush soundscape. The distinctive 'lifeguard whistle' of the Varied Thrush pierced the peace now and again. Welcome, once we confirmed it was not a stranded hiker's alert.

Kayaking on near-freezing Lake Mendenhall to its bespoke glacier and nearby cascade was magical. Touching a small iceberg's silky surface gave peaceful contrast to dodging the hysterically erratic steering of another kayak. And those ferry rides criss-crossing Lynn Canal and Glacier Bay! Concerns that 'mundane' or repeated travel modes would detract from 'real' activities faded as from the ferry deck, we drank in panoramas teeming with wildlife. With patience, we saw sea lions, otters with pups, puffins, whale spouts, bears, bald eagles, mountain goats with kids, artic terns, dolphins and porpoises.

Even the imperfections worked out. When a canceled ferry imploded expensive plans, our revised train ride to White Pass freed time for an unplanned hike. Cruise ships offloaded crowds, but the floating skyscrapers were fascinating contrasts to view (briefly!) against the natural setting. Moose remained elusive to all but one of us, but his thrill was contagious. The 40-mile bike ride to the bald eagle reserve in Haines included 10+ miles of pouring rain, just one eagle, and bike trouble, but the bike rental fee was waived, trumpeter swans decorated our ride, and afterward dozens of bald eagles swooped past our lodgings for days. The Hammer Museum excited just one of us but the story will entertain each of us forever. From aboard a public bus, Juneau's work-a-day practicalities obscured nearby vistas. Yet, commuters heartily thanking the driver upon disembarking was a delightful custom we joined.

Alaska is over-sized and amazing. I still cannot believe I was there. Yet this is not some humble-brag travel log. It's a friendly reminder that even if the scale of your summer outings is more local than Alaskan, you can take a chance, embrace conditions, enjoy wonder, learn from the details, curry resolutions, and share your experiences with others.

## PONDER & POST

Alaska is a big state, but a small town.
Anon

In Alaska, I found a wilderness that touched my soul and filled me with awe and reverence for the natural world.
John Muir

Moose are the squirrels of Alaska.
Anon

In Alaska, you can go out your door and be in a completely different world.
Bear Grylls

Some people look for a beautiful place. Others make a place beautiful.
Hazrat Inayat Khan

The magic thing about home is that it feels good to leave, and it feels even better to come back.
Wendy Wunder

## PRACTICAL | PROACTIVE | PRO-COMMUNITY

### Start Simple & Spread Out
*Stay-cations & Armchair Traveling*

There's no place like home. Yet a proper stay-cation means experiencing the familiar in new ways. Try this:

1. Plan the details as carefully as if you were leaving town. Schedule both active and down times.

2. Time or money restrictions require thoughtful, creative budgeting – not a default to stinginess or moping.

3. Avoid the beaten path. Go to one new place each day. Grocery store or a grander locale – just try something new.

4. Go camping or glamping in your backyard one night. Or at least make s'mores at a (borrowed?) firepit under starlight.

5. Host a global film festival, one per several nights. Or try a rainy-day marathon. Select at least one film per continent. Aim for family friendly titles that suit a range of tastes or needs. Try movies that inspire travel like *Up, Moana, Chronicles of Narnia, Finding Nemo, The Secret Life of Walter Mitty*. Or movies that bring the world to you like *Best Exotic Marigold Hotel, Chasing Liberty, North of the Sun, Long Way Down, Madagascar, The Gods Must Be Crazy, The Last Holiday, The Endless Summer*. Don't forget documentaries like Attenborough's *Africa* or *Panamericana - Life at the Longest Road on Earth*. Enjoy snacks to match each film's culture or theme.

### Go Big & Go Home!

*Host a Travel-Inspired Potluck Gathering*

This activity scales easily from just a few family members or friends to a team or club event to a neighborhood street party. Start small with a handful of cooks then do it again with a bigger group.

Pick a date and send an invitation something like this:

## WHAT'S GOOD to EAT WHERE YOU'VE GONE?
*(or where you'd like to go)*

Join us for a potluck picnic gathering!
[insert date / location / time]
RSVP to [name/email] by [date]

**SHARE YOUR TASTES IN TRAVEL!** Bring an appetizer, easy-to-eat entree, or dessert that represents your favorite (or dream) destination. Prepare enough to serve 6-8 people. Include a place card with the name of your food, where it's from, any key or unusual ingredients, and the reason you like the food and/or where it came from so much.

**BYO adult beverages and outdoor chairs (optional). Host will provide:** [insert things like 1-2 basic beverages/water; plates, napkins & utensils; covered tables; lighting]

Option: Let folks know you will collect donations for a well-vetted nonprofit that fights hunger. The money could go towards clearing the lunch debt accrued by students at a local school, to a group serving in your county like Meals on Wheels or a soup kitchen/pantry, or to an international initiative like Haiti Health Promise (https://crudem.org/).

## PROMPTS

*Wonder – Write – What Next?*

In *The Wizard of Oz* Dorothy fervently swears, "There's no place like home." Of course, she does have quite an adventure to convince her of this. In *Toy Story* Buzz Lightyear eagerly proclaims, "To infinity and beyond!" yet never strays too far from his friends. F. Scott Fitzgerald launched the 'two things can be true at once' concept with, "The test of a first-rate intelligence is the ability to hold two opposed ideas in mind at the same time and still retain the ability to function."

So, are you a 'get-me-home' Dorothy? An 'I'm outta here' Buzz? Or are you with Fitzgerald and happy to balance both?

I'm DOROTHY when/if:

    1.

    2.

    3.

I'm BUZZ when/if:

    1.

    2.

    3.

Two opposite things that are true about me as a traveler are:

    1.

    2.

The PERFECT week-long vacation for me would look like this (sketch or list):

# Summer Daze

H ello, Neighbors!

The hottest month of summer, August in the northern hemisphere, is a great month for doing nothing. Or at least nothing that's too routine. In August we can loll and linger. Let new ideas simmer as we store up energy for a busy fall.

There are so many ways to indulge in hot, lazy, hazy days. Like… Shifting to catch any hint of a breeze. Slurping icy beverages or ice cream, such blissful contrasts to high heat and humidity. Drowsing in the shade for a break. Plunging into pools, ponds, oceans, or sprinkler spray. Dropping an ice cube down your shirt. Shivering in the AC after work or play is done.

Chores don't disappear, of course. Yet even the laundry's easier since t-shirts and shorts dry and fold much quicker than winter's many layers. Landscaping tasks may let up as the grass and hopefully some weeds dial down during dry spells. Yet even if the season's prodigal flurry of blooms and growth goes unchecked, there's time to stop and smell the roses…and those heavenly magnolia blossoms.

August might include the engine whines of nearby yard or home renovation projects. Yet even the most industrious crews slow to a pace demanded by outdoor conditions. Evenings have their own noise. Kids shout as they play in yards, on ball fields, or at the pool. Bugs hum, buzz, and chur. Night creatures claim space. Eventually, the quiet comes and it's time to be dazzled by lightning bug shows or starlit vistas.

August may be a tipping point for hectic things to come, but they're not here yet.

Savor these redolent days.

## PONDER & POST

Deep summer is when laziness finds respectability.
Sam Keen

Summer is singing with joy, and the beaches are inviting you with dancing waves.
Debasish Mridha

Rest is not idleness, and to lie sometimes on the grass on a summer day listening to the murmur of water, or watching the clouds float across the sky, is hardly a waste of time.
John Lubbock

Summer means happy times and good sunshine.
>Brian Wilson

Summer night – even the stars are whispering to each other.
>Kobayashi Issa

Roll out those lazy, hazy, crazy days of summer.
>1st recorded by Nat King Cole

Summer has filled her veins with light and her heart is washed with noon.
>C. Day Lewis

A perfect summer day is when the sun is shining, the breeze is blowing, the birds are singing, & the lawnmower is broken.
>James Dent

Shall I compare thee to a summer's day?
>William Shakespeare

Some of the best memories are made in flip-flops.
>Kellie Elmore

> It's a smile, it's a kiss, it's a sip of wine…It's summertime!
> — Kenny Chesney

> …Maintain a little bit of summer, even in the middle of winter.
> — Henry David Thoreau

> There shall be eternal summer in the grateful heart.
> — Celia Thaxter

## PRACTICAL | PROACTIVE | PRO-COMMUNITY

### Start Simple & Spread Out
*Simple-Yet-Special Melon & Mint Summer Salad*

If you're growing mint, you know there's always plenty to share in season. If you don't have fresh mint, give fresh lemon balm a go. Add watermelon for a colorful melon trifecta. Travels well for picnics. Multiply proportions for a pretty, refreshing dish to share at a summer gathering.

Ingredients (serves 4+)

1 cantaloupe
1 honeydew melon
5-6 medium mint leaves (fresh)
optional: 1-2 TBSP simple syrup OR orange juice

Use a melon ball scoop for even, rounded bites. To get every melon morsel, try slicing and cubing instead.
Mix together fruit and optional syrup/juice in a large bowl. The fruit looks pretty in a white or dark blue bowl.
Tear mint leaves to large flake sized. Lightly stir into melon mix. Save some to sprinkle on top.

Serve chilled, especially on really hot days.

### Go Big & Go Home!

#### *Water Frolics with Family & Friends*

Test these activities first with just 1-2 people. Try them one at a time or in bunches to see how each suits your age group and interests. Then set up for a day of soggy silliness with at least four stations. Invite folks to wear bathing suits and sneakers that can get wet – flip flops & slippery antics don't mix well. Set rules to meet skill and/or age levels – prioritize fun over finesse. Assign an adult or capable teen as 'fun guards' at each station (whistles optional).

Water Squirters

- Target Practice - Make or choose a hoop to shoot water through. Suspend it with string so it hangs close to eye level. Try a big hole (hula hoop) for small or new players. Shrink according to abilities or age (inner tube, ring toss hoop). Post a 'judge' if you want to make sure the streams of water make it through the target hole.

- Rubber Duckie Race - Fill a baby pool with ~5 inches of water. Wedge two pool noodles across the diameter to make one long lane. Players take turns placing one duck in the lane and using only the stream of their water squirter to move the rubber duckie to the other side. Who can get a rubber duckies across the kiddie pool in the fewest number of squirts or refills?

- Swing Soak – One person swings on a regular swing, tire swing, or rope (tire swing works best). Everyone else squirts-to-soak. Take turns! Mark a clear line on the ground that squirters must stand behind (to avoid arc of the swing). Control chaos by limiting it to 1-3 squirters per round.

Ice Cubes

- Floating Glaciers – Each player stands at a 5-gallon bucket filled 3/4 with water. Add the same number of ice cubes to each bucket. Give players the same sized spoon or scoop. Who can remove the ice cubes first into a discard bowl? Increase the challenge with smaller spoons, fewer cubes (floating more freely), and rules like 'scoop only one piece of ice at a time.'

- Ice-n-Spoon Race – Runners race to a finish line while holding out a spoon with an ice cube in it (like an egg-n-spoon race). Harder options include no holding the ice onto the spoon with a free hand or the runner must return to the start line if the ice drops.

- Melting Contest – Give each player one same-sized cube in a small paper cup. Who can make the cube melt first? How about without touching it? Tip: Decide for each round if the cube can be removed from the cup.

Water Balloons (half-filled)

- Toss Across – Pair off. Give one half-filled water balloon to each pair. Partners toss and catch the balloon, taking one step backwards after each successful catch. The winning pair has the intact balloon AND farthest distance apart after 10 steps, 5 minutes, OR 'last-one standing' status. Option: final partners have a 'toss off' to determine the ultimate single champ.

- Batting Practice – Offer a bucket of half-filled water balloons. Players use a toddler or whiffle ball bat to hit pitched balloons. Experiment with self-pitch, soft underhand pitch, and hitting off a tee. Optional – Outfielders can try to catch the hits.

Water Balloons (large)

- Pinata – Hang a pinata that is made from a large, water-filled balloon. Take turns hitting or offer several balloo-natas for a mass smash-off. One person per well-spaced pinata, please!

- Balloon Grating – Fill a large water balloon almost all the way. Draw a clear line with permanent marker around the balloon's diameter, at least halfway down from the top knot. Time to play! The player lays face up on a mat, bench, lounge chair, or cot. The Balloon Master holds the balloon (knot end up) in two hands with minimal squeezing ~6 inches above a player's face. The player uses a hand-held cheese grater to rub the balloon three times per turn. The player can grate anywhere below the marked line for each turn. Take turns Jenga-style. The 'winner' is the one who gets wet when the series of shared gratings finally breaches the balloon. Best for 3 or more players.

Sprinkles & Sprays

- Classic Fun – A simple sprinkler can be a ton of fun. Just watch the hose layout (tripping) and the water pressure (blasting faces). Give extra room away from other play spaces for uncharted running around.

- Yes You Can – Gather small watering cans and a trough or baby pool filled with water. Invite youngsters to scoop, fill, and pour. It's fun to water plants, stones, the fence, tree trunks, each, etc. Pouring into other containers of all sizes spread around the pool is fun, too. And if you're okay with muddy messes – just add dirt.

- Water Paints – Offer a collection of new (or at least very clean) paint brushes in all sizes and buckets of water. Invite players to 'paint' the fence, the car, the porch posts, or even their own skin. Option: Designate and/or contain an area. Add chalk and let artists make water and chalk designs on the sidewalk, driveway, or stockade fence. Too messy? Paint them out with water-only brushes. Or let that team of sprinklers take over.

- Up & Over – Set up two lines of chairs, front to back; use at least 4 chairs per row. Provide a full bucket or bowl of water for each row. Size the container so it's mildly challenging to lift up, overhead, and behind until the next person in the row takes it. The rows race to lift the water-filled container from first to last chair. Winners have the most water at the end. Set a time limit or require three rounds to increase the challenge. This is similar to 2014's viral fundraiser, the Ice Bucket Challenge for ALS, but the goal is to NOT tip out the water (and no ice needed).

## PROMPTS

### *Wonder – Write – What Next?*

List the 5 Water Frolics that will work best in your setting. Annotate with a shopping or gathering list.

1.

2.

3.

4.

5.

Measure your yard (or chosen Frolic setting) then plan the layout of the stations you've selected. Consider which ones need a running hose, room to run, or structures for hanging things. Sketch the optimal layout here.

# Second Chances

**H**ello, Neighbors!

For years, there was an old and untended house next door. It had been a family home for decades, then it was subdivided (awkwardly) as a rental for new adults working their first jobs. After that, it stood empty, subject to weather and animal invasion for a very long time. Last year, the old manse finally was sold and eventually torn down by a professional building company. Four busy months later, and one bright and very 'big-i-nized' new home is here! As the long-time homeowner across the street from the new colossus joked about her classic and tidy brick rambler, "Do they know the main view is just my little house?"

In other words, the rebuild is rather grand – with a list price to match. It also is pretty. And packed with lots of lovely features that should attract a family who enjoys entertaining – starting with that kitchen. So, while I'll always miss the large trees sacrificed for the job, the rebuilding process and the result remind me that second chances - even loud, prolonged, or messy ones - can turn out better than anticipated.

To recap, the old house probably was disintegrating from underground with mold and more in the mix. But it didn't really bother anyone on the street. We even appreciated how its overgrown yard became a haven for spring fawns and occasional foxes. So when it sold, we braced for chaos. Yes, we had jack hammers, big trucks, and porta-potties. But we also had working crews who parked considerately, were very efficient, and cleaned up, sometimes in big ways. To wit, when neighbors were planning an outdoor party for a milestone event, they requested 'something' to address their ugly view of the worksite. Without fuss or delay, the crew spruced the adjacent unfinished façade with new paint and removed all heavy equipment from the site. Later, when another neighbor was struggling with the billion leaves spilling off her curb, three of the work crew swooped in to gather and haul away everything. And those homeowners with adjacent lots? They aren't mad about getting a long-term reprieve from replacing their own (some already jenky) fence lines, thanks to the new property's spiffy stockade border.

Did it take time? Were there ugly moments and painful losses? Did it disgruntle some forest friends and other natives? Yes, yes, and yes. And yes, the result will take some getting used to. Oh, there's nothing bad about the pristine white siding and black-trimmed windows. The landscaping is complete; its small plants will fill out soon. Inside, the engineering and technology should be top-notch, too. So, we'll absorb the changes and look forward to what the new neighbors bring.

Speaking of changes, construction often includes dealing with materials no longer suitable for the given build site. Landscaping can be moved or mulched, but there's more to consider. Owners of houses and other structures getting a second chance should consider services like the non-profit, Second Chance, Inc. They manage deconstructing – versus demolishing - a home. The team assesses what's salvageable and helps to repurpose or sell the materials for reuse. The process can bring tax and other benefits, too.

As a community-building bonus, Second Chance hires displaced and unemployed people who get a re-start that includes training to work in deconstruction. Based in Baltimore, MD, and easily accessible to the Washington, DC metro area, Second Chance can facilitate sustainability for resource-hungry projects. And careers for some perhaps under-supported people. Win, win! If you're not building but just sprucing up, shop at Habitat for Humanity's ReStores or other local iterations like the Second Chance shop in Baltimore for materials gleaned and/or repurposed by experts for reuse by most anyone needing building supplies.

If your metro area is nowhere near Baltimore just enter 'deconstruction and reuse services near [city name] area metro' in your search engine for some solid choices. If you don't get any hits, contact Habitat for Humanity, Second Chance, or another deconstruction services company in the closest big city for leads on who can help closer to your zip code. Feeling some DIY? See budgetdumpster.com/blog/home-deconstruction-guide for a professional-grade overview with clear principles, goals, and tips for managing your own deconstruction and reuse.

Of course, there's more to restoration than physical shelter and design. For those of you facing totally different categories of complex rebuilding, your second chances are out there, too. With plenty of 'change orders,' off-beat timing, and unexpected twists to manage. Like all quality (re-)building, you'll need to seek basic, practical help to stay the course. Recruit experts who truly listen, care, and follow up. Check with neighbors – new and old – for insights and recommendations. You can do it.

Here's to firm foundations, distinct choices, and clear goals - no matter what new doors or windows you seek.

## PONDER & POST

When one door closes, another opens.
Alexander Graham Bell

If I had a hammer
I'd hammer in the morning
I'd hammer in the evening
All over this land
I'd hammer out danger
I'd hammer out a warning
I'd hammer out love between
My brothers and my sisters
All over this land
Pete Seeger & Lee Hays, sung by Peter, Paul, & Mary

## PRACTICAL | PROACTIVE | PRO-COMMUNITY

### Start Simple & Spread Out
*Good Fences Make Good Neighbors*

There aren't a lot of traditional Amish builders living in the suburbs of big cities. So, shared barn- and fence-building is not really a thing there. Suburbanites yet to master boarder building and maintenance can try these tips of Posthole Digger Diplomacy.

1. The unwritten rules of Fence Manners suggest that the 'pretty' or finished side of the fence should face out. This may seem obvious for the streetscape, but it's less intuitive to do it for side and back borders, too. But thems the rules. Happily, there are designs that look finished on both sides.

2. Don't skimp. Dig the holes deep. Pour the concrete generously. Use the right hardware. It really does help with longevity, especially anywhere the ground freezes, or shakes, or high winds blow through. Got gates? Consider three, long strap hinges over just two of most any other style.

3. Be street legal. You may need permits (pro installers can handle this) or at least HOA permission. Call utility companies to mark their lines BEFORE you dig. Make sure you're building on your own property; check the survey or plat. Most municipalities own a strip of land along the street; check public records. You can build on it, but you may have to move the fence (at your expense) should the local ordinances for the drainage system or curb structures change.

4. Communicate. Minimally, let adjacent neighbors know a few weeks ahead of time about your plans to build a fence. Even better, ask said neighbors to collaborate on the shared border's fence style and budget. Should one household want to update in 10+ years, remember who did (or did not) opt to collaborate the first time. Later, budget and design accordingly.

5. Stockade is great for very private backyard boarders. It may serve a purpose around front, too. But be ready for kids to say yours is 'the Scary

House' on the street if your fence seems to be hiding something.

6. For lower fences, choose pickets that are close enough to prevent dogs or small kids from squeezing in or busting out. Also, build high enough to discourage jumping or climbing out, but good luck if you have a Springer Spaniel or a very dexterous toddler. If you like a rail fence, consider lining it with chicken or hog wire metal fencing for the same containment reasons. For a refined look, wire mesh painted black tends to disappear from view.

7. Technically, in most places it's legal for homeowners to trim plants overhanging a fence into their yard. Nonetheless, should botany intrude don't just whack off offending parts (*the tree's*) without first asking the neighbor about easy or at least mutually agreeable solutions.

8. It's a fence not a demilitarized zone. Meet frequently at the shared fence line. Chat about the weather. Exchange landscaping tips or extra plants. Invite each other – or at least the kids – over to play.

**Go Big & Go Home!**

*Plant for Pollinators*

Good landscaping makes for pretty streets and happy passers-by. And by good, I don't mean manicured like a golf course. I mean planted with an array of varied native flora that attract 6-legged and winged admirers of all sorts. Good landscapes are replete with bees, butterflies, moths, beetles, ladybugs, and so many other small-but-mighty, industrious beings that are busy, busy, busy on everyone's behalf. So, as you organize your garden layout and bloom times, do what you can to benefit the creepy-crawly community organizers that keep your yard blooming as just part of their life-giving work.

Plan your landscape – or even just that one pot by your front door – to ensure successful growth. If you pick the right plant for the conditions of your yard, you often can 'set it then forget it' once the roots take hold.

The Plant Hardiness Zone or number is the first step. Find your hardiness zone @ planthardiness.ars.usda.gov/. They offer a US map color-coded by zones and hardiness numbers as well as a search window to find growing-related basics by zip code. You'll find the hardiness number and color-coded map on seed packets, plant catalogue blurbs, and garden center signs, too. Use them to select annuals and perennials that will be happy at your house year-round.

Next, take note of your yard's shade vs. sun, soil type, and your watering preferences to pick the perfect varieties to plant. Read plant tags, then match your conditions to the plant's needs. Feeling fancy? Check bloom times and install plants so you have flowers, berries, etc. from early spring to late fall (or longer if it's warm year-round). Pollinators love (and need) flowers, so here are just a few loyal, easy-care residents of the Plantae community:

- Full-sun Flowers – Zinnias thrive most anywhere from summer into fall. Their eye-catching petals appeal to people and pollinators alike. Easy seeders and happy in direct sun, they are great for cutting gardens. Lavender, Geraniums, Petunias, and Pinks (dianthus) are long-lived sun-seekers with constant blooms, too.

- Shady Characters – Try Hellebore (early spring), Begonia (summer), Astilbe (into the fall), and Impatiens (all warm-season long). Liriope and Creeping Myrtle are great blooming groundcovers. Fuchsias and Coleus like hanging baskets and pots, too.

- Trees & Shrubs – Most trees flower early. Red Bud, Pear, Cherry Blossom, and Dogwood trees provide an early and much-needed spring welcome. Mimosas and Magnolias follow as the weather warms. Azalea bushes once decorated only the spring, but the ever-blooming varieties really do stick around. Hydrangea start popping by early summer and, if watered, their big, bouncy blooms add cheer well past Labor Day.

Got mosquitoes, nibs, or gnats? They play key roles in keeping our ecosystems thriving. Instead of automatically and aggressively un-aliving those bugs that seem most pesty, try these alternatives first.

- Plant night-blooming flowers that don't attract pollinators during daytime playtime.

- Time your blooming plants to hit peak when you're traveling. Stay-cationers will love the view in your stead.

- Install bat houses. If the buzzy pests have just got to go, let your friendly, neighborhood bats take advantage.

- Use carefully placed, liquid traps. Search 'safe liquid bug traps' online for commercial options. DIY with an upcycled plastic bottle, some apple cider vinegar or lemon juice, and a dash of dish soap to trap those that come closest to your outdoor seating area.

- Avoid zappers or sticky things that attract even the innocent winged things, often with cruel results.

- Light natural oil-based sticks or spirals with smoke that deters pests.

- Wear bug-repelling bracelets or clothes.

- If you must spray, try those made with citrus, soap, or citronella. Experiment with time of day, frequency, spacing, and density of application for sufficient human relief but minimal over-spraying of your bevy of beneficial bugs.

## PROMPTS

### *Wonder – Write – What Next?*

Your Dream Home – List 3 features of any sort that top your list of Must Haves in a new or renovated home.

1.

2.

3.

Your Dream Street – List 3 features of any sort that top your list of Must Haves for updating your street.

1.

2.

3.

Your Dream Town – List 3 features of any sort that top you list of Must Haves for updating your town.

1.

2.

3.

Star one feature per list that is MOST achievable by this time next year. Name one person to ask for help on making ONE of these updates happen:


Define the first step to take to make ONE of these updates happen:

# THE TAYLOR SWIFT EFFECT

Hello, Neighbors!

Remember the Eras Tour of 2023-24? When Taylor Swift blew the doors off concert culture by selling out night after night after night all over the world? Already globally renowned for her "versatile musicality, songwriting prowess, and business acuity" (Wikipedia) *before* this tour, Swift was equally established as charitable force, ranking third most generous on a 2022 list of celebrity philanthropists. And during Eras she robustly funded foodbanks in every city where she performed. Talk about 'value added!'

That concept applies to Swift in traditional economic terms, too, and at various scales. Starting small-ish, there's the swift trade in friendship bracelets she's inspired, more boon than blip to craft suppliers and markets everywhere. Then as *Bloomberg Economics* notes, the Eras Tour contributed $4.3 billion to the US GDP, thanks to heavy use in urban areas of hospitality services like hotels, local businesses, and tourism. At the time, this amount is larger than the GDP of ~50 countries.

Why feature Swift in a book that celebrates local living? Well, for one, plenty of Swifties live in small places. Sure, some scored tickets to an Eras concert. But limited supply (Swift physically can do only so many shows), the $49-$450 cost per ticket (some re-sold for $1,000+), and/or the EPIC online ticket sale snafu meant a cruel summer for the many hopefuls left at home. The cumulative impact of those disgruntled fans who were scattered across countless households created other, bigger changes.

First, look at ticket sale policies. Ticketmaster was ready to accommodate 1.5 million fans for the first day of online presales. Fourteen million logged in to buy and the sight crashed. Beyond unsnarling the tech failures, US lawmakers launched congressional inquiries, including an antitrust investigation. Among other responses, ticket platforms for music and across hospitality categories eliminated many of their so-called 'service' and 'convenience' fees. Scalping bots that jacked up pricing or at least lessened access were banned, too. One legal scholar called this serious response "the Taylor Swift policy adjustment."

Civic securities also were refined and upgraded when threats of stalkers or harm to female fans increased at certain intervals or locales. Internationally, political leaders demanded fair updates to ticketing policies and similar legally relevant processing. Some government representatives 'demanded' Swift perform in all their major cities in hopes of economic benefits. Others provided 'grants' to support the tour traveling great distances. Some asked Swift to encourage voter participation in national elections.

The point is, amid all the global fanfare and fried nerves, Taylor's version of a response included fostering local support for regular folk. For example, Taylor's team quickly released *Taylor Swift: The Eras Tour,* the concert film, in theaters all over the United States. Born in small-town West Reading, PA, Swift's plan to expedite this documentary's release was not a quick money grab. The film would sell out whenever it was ready. Releasing quickly showed inherent respect for the 'micro-economics' of some people's entertainment and travel budgets, not to mention the relative scarcity of tickets to the live shows.

On a larger scale and having already shaken off billionaire behemoths of the recording industry, Swift remained mindful of the then-unresolved WGA/SGA-AFTRA creatives' rights strike against Hollywood's mega-studios. She and her team chose to distribute *Taylor Swift: The Eras Tour* at as close to a grassroots level as her generous endeavors can operate. Meaning, local theater owners and their many local employees got to bring the live tour's sparkle to local Swifties happy to experience the concert in its right-sized-for-here form.

Whether or not you're a Swiftie, she's a great reminder to love what you do and share it in ways that nurture and respect the economic opportunities, social capital, and personal connections you can foster within your sphere of influence. Better still, is doing so while dancing.

## PONDER & POST

From Taylor

> Oh, I'm just a girl trying to find a place in this world.
> (*A Place in the World*)

> This ain't Hollywood, this is a small town... (*White Horse*)

> I love my hometown as much as Motown... (*London Boy*)

> You can change your style, you can change your jeans
> You can learn to fly, and you can chase your dreams
> You can laugh and cry, but everybody knows
> You'll always find your way back home
> (*You'll Always Find Your Way Back Home*)

> No matter what happens in life, be good to people. Being good to people is a wonderful legacy to leave behind.

Jot your favorite 'hometown Taylor' lyric(s) here:

About Taylor

> But for all that globe-trotting, there are some artists that you see do a show and you know they don't even know what city they're in. I always feel like Taylor knows exactly where she is. She has a relationship with that city or that market and those fans and she's connected to them in ways that are very authentic, that you can't fake.
>
> Bernie Cahill (music manager)

## PRACTICAL | PROACTIVE | PRO-COMMUNITY

### Start Simple & Spread Out
*Friendship Bracelets*

Gather your beads, thread, and patience! It's time to craft. There are maybe a zillion ways to design and make friendship bracelets. Do what you know or what moves you. If you want to try Swiftie style (exchanging them was ALL the rage for fans EVERYWHERE during the Eras Tour), then enter 'Swiftie friendship bracelets' in a search engine for inspiration. Most of them are a combination of colorful beads and letters that spell out happy terms and/or references to her lyrics, albums a.k.a. eras, or the tour. After you make your own, you can...

- Personalize the bracelets for family and friends with their own name or those of pets, hobbies, teams, etc.

- Create a theme bracelet for a family reunion, graduation party, team event, or vacation trip. Make one for everyone or bring supplies for a DIY group gathering.

- Drop off a batch at a local hospital with designs that medical staff would appreciate like, *I* [heart bead] *health*, *I am vital*, or short puns related to various job titles. Or create bracelets with cute animal beads or cheery words like *strong*, *feisty*, or *looking good* for staff to hand out to patients.

**Go Big & Go Home!**

*Host an Eras Tour Film Festival*

Be like Taylor. Get everyone singing, dancing, and having fun. Project the *Taylor Swift: The Eras Tour* concert film in a place where folks can party. Consider a roomy basement, anywhere you can hang a sheet securely, a white garage door, or in the event room of a community center or library. Notify the local Swifties that you'll be screening The Eras Tour movie and everyone's invited to come – decked out in the 'Taylor era' of their choice, of course.

Be like Taylor. Give stuff away. Spread the joy of the event with a charitable donation element. Consider asking attendees for optional contributions of cash, canned goods, or other items specifically listed by your local food bank, shelter, or equivalent. For more funds, set up various stations and charge $1 per use or $5 for a 'premium pass' (stamp or wristband) to all stations. Accept cash and Venmo or similar.

1. Selfie Station: Balloon arch with concert props, including a life-sized cutout of Taylor Swift.

2. Bracelet Station: Bead those bracelets to wear and share!

3. Lyrics Graffiti Mural: Mount large poster board or bulletin board paper on a flat surface. Provide markers or similar and let the artists add their favorite song lyric. Doodles encouraged. Post pics of the final mural to socials with #taylorswift, #taylorswiftconcert, #missamerica, #taylorswiftsongs or any of your favorites. Consider adding a donations link & explanation if you include fundraising at your event.

## PROMPTS

### *Wonder – Write – What Next?*

Are you a Swiftie? Prove it!
(or grab your favorite Swiftie and be enlightened)

My favorite TS ERA is
because...


My favorite TS SONG is
because...


My favorite TS LYRIC is


because...


My favorite TS FUN FACT is


because...


If you are not a Swiftie yet, what's holding you back?

Taylor Swift isn't the only gal with a penchant for boosting economics while stirring up her own kind of good trouble. An intrepid tooth fairy named Gwyneth shares all kinds of big ideas for young minds in this picture book for all ages, *Gwyneth & the Flossy Posse*.

Plaque Man is back! And he's spreading rotten advice like, 'Want sweet dreams? Eat candy in bed,' 'Need more sleep? Skip flossing!' Gwyneth finds these notes along her tooth collection route and she's ready to floss & toss the gunky foe. Gwyneth heads to Tooth Con to find help polishing off Plaque Man. But the other tooth fairies don't believe he's trying to ruin the very teeth they collect to save, spend, and share in the tooth fairy world. Ignoring the doubters, Gwyneth learns dental defense tips from experts like Mr. Buck Touffe and Dr. Claire N. Wight. And when Plaque Man launches a direct attack at Tooth Con, Gwyneth is ready to rally a flossy posse with enough mental and dental derring-do to wash him down the drain.

You haven't met Gwyneth yet, but try predicting 3 ways she treats fans, peers, and the occasional baddie in her tooth fairy world. How similar might she be to Taylor Swift?

1. With fans, I predict Gwyneth…

2. With peers, I predict Gwyneth…

3. With baddies, I predict Gwyneth…

Repurpose some Taylor Swift lyrics to...

A) Present what Taylor may think of or do about Plaque Man's ill treatment of kids and tooth fairies like Gwyneth

B) Write an anthem for Gwyneth to sing with the Flossy Posse as they take down Plaque Man

# HOLD THE APOSTROPHE

H ello, Neighbors!

As an editor, I like sharing that Veterans Day does not use an apostrophe. This is because the day is not one that belongs just to veterans. Rather, Veterans Day is for all of us. Yes, it's to honor those who have served honorably in the military during war or peace – on behalf of everyone. Veterans Day is <u>not</u> just for military personnel to congratulate or commiserate with each other. Instead, the day is for showing appreciation <u>to</u> veterans for their contributions to national security and the sacrifices they've made while fulfilling their duty. To clarify further, living veterans are the main focus of Veterans Day since Memorial Day commemorates others.

As a long-time, adjacent-to-DC local, I was not surprised to learn of Congress's changeable approach to enacting Veterans Day as a formal holiday. November 11 was first called Armistice Day to honor the official end of World War 1. In 1938, Congress made it a legal holiday. The Act of 1938 was amended in 1954 to replace "Armistice" with "Veterans." Congress attempted to consolidate federal holidays to Mondays starting in 1968. The ensuing confusion pushed Veterans Day back to October 25 in 1971. President Gerald Ford restored the original date in 1978. The Veterans Day National Ceremony, now always on November 11 at 11 a.m., includes wreath laying at the Tomb of the Unknown Soldier and a parade of colors in the nation's capital.

As a busy person who likes choices and chances, it's good to know additional days to honor veterans include Medal of Honor Day (3/25), Vietnam Veterans

Day (3/29), Former POW Recognition Day (4/9), Armed Forces Day(5/20), Women Veterans Day (6/12), Korean War Veterans Armistice Day (7/27), Purple Heart Day (7/7), and Pearl Harbor Remembrance Day (12/7).

As a citizen who has benefited from others' military service, I'm impressed by the volume that has been provided. In 2023, 18.5 million or 6.1 percent of American adults were veterans. Sixteen million Americans served in WWII with about 61,256 still alive in 2025. Korean War veterans totaled 1.8 million, 2.7million people served in the Vietnam War, and there were 650,000 serving in the Gulf War. As of May 2025, the U.S. Army, Navy, Marine Corps, Air Force, Space Force, and Coast Guard have a combined 1.3 million active-duty service members and 762,000 reserve and national guard members. [1]

As an educator, I hope the depth and decorum of Veterans Day get shared across generations. Search https://department.va.gov for 'Veterans Day Facts, Information, Teaching Resources' or any browser for 'Veterans Day & Kids' to find youth-friendly ways to show appreciation to veterans. Adults may appreciate the insights gleaned from books like *The Women* by Kristin Hannah, *Once An Eagle* by Anton Myrer, or *The Things They Carried* by Tim O'Brien.

As a reader of this essay, perhaps you relate to Veterans Day similarly or even more personally. Either way, there are plenty of veterans in our midst who have served and sacrificed for our country and community. So hold the apostrophe, not the gratitude. This Veterans Day – or any day, really – find a service member and say thank you.

---

1. US Census Bureau, Dept. of Veteran Affairs, Dept. of Defense

## PONDER & POST

No duty is more urgent than that of returning thanks.
James Allen

Honor to the soldier and sailor everywhere, who bravely bears his country's cause. Honor, also, to the citizen who cares for his brother in the field and serves, as he best can, the same cause.
Abraham Lincoln

In valor there is hope.
Publius Cornelius Tacitus

Peace has its victories, but it takes brave men and women to win them.
Ralph Waldo Emerson

Freedom is not free.
Walter Hitchcock

Scared is what you're feeling. Brave is what you're doing.
Emma Donoghue

How far that little candle throws his beams! So shines a good deed in a naughty world.
William Shakespeare

The strength of a nation derives from the integrity of the home.
Confucious

There is nothing stronger than the heart of a volunteer.
Jimmy Doolittle

He loves his country best who strives to make It best.
Robert G. Ingersoll

The soldier above all others prays for peace, for it is the soldier who must suffer and bear the deepest wounds and scars of war.
Douglas MacArthur

True heroism is remarkably sober, very undramatic. It is not the urge to surpass all others at whatever cost, but the urge to serve others at whatever cost.
Arthur Ashe

All the great things are simple, and many can be expressed in a single word: freedom, justice, honor, duty, mercy, hope.
Winston Churchill

Ask not what your country can do for you — ask what you can do for your country.
John F. Kennedy

## PRACTICAL | PROACTIVE | PRO-COMMUNITY

### Start Simple & Spread Out
*Service-Minded Songs*

Create a playlist that highlights the merits, sacrifices, and/or processes of service. Your selections may lean toward the patriotic (*God Bless the U.S.A.*, Lee Greenwood), the familiar (*Take Me Home, Country Roads*, John Denver), the inspiring (Hero, Mariah Carey), the spiritual (song), the street (*Unity in Community*, Leo Mercer).

Just want to jam, but not plan? See Spotify's playlist called 'Songs about Community' which ranges from *We're All In This Together* (*High School Musical*) to *One Love* (Bob Marley) to *Power of the People* (Monster Truck).

### Go Big & Go Home!

*Creative Messaging*

Art has always influenced community. Those prehistoric cave paintings of herd animals discovered in France depicted realities useful to survival. Countless statues and paintings over the centuries have highlighted virtues and served to influence and inspire people. Some modern-era artists quite intentionally present art with messages of activism or calls to service.

In the spirit of 'artists giving back,' the blogging team at Arteral.com shared *Spotlight on 9 Artists Who Practice The Art of Giving*. It's worth checking out the brief blurbs on artists influencing the art market with direct resources for creative initiatives that benefit organizations serving those with serious needs. Banksy, the pseudonym for a British street artist who lately confirms he will answer to Robbie, is a similarly proactive creator. A popular visual compendium of the artist's work is available in Antonelli & Marziani's photo book, *Banksy*.

Audiences of most any age can learn about Banksy with Fausto Gilberti's picture book, *Banksy Graffitied Walls and Wasn't Sorry*.

Since the 1990s, Banksy has melded his stencil and graffiti-based work with permanent fixtures in public spaces like streets, walls, and bridges across the globe. His identity remains shrouded (he installs without legal permissions), but his impacts are world-famous. He has intentionally helped many service-oriented organizations and charities sell his guerilla installations in order to raise funds for their own programming. Hailing from Bristol, in 2014 he installed a mural on the doors of a youth club struggling to stay open. Officials confiscated the illegal installation, so Banksy granted the youth shelter ownership of the mural. The shelter sold the mural for an estimated £400,000 which sustained the shelter. Banksy watchers are convinced this was what the local boy turned famous artist always intended.

Not everyone can or should be Banksy, but it's okay to create with some of his energy and intent. How?

1. Pick a spot on your own property or elsewhere with (preferably written) permission of the owner. Think shed, side door, swing, or sidewalk. Building facades, pedestrian bridges, and the like require official processes and permits, but if your plan is solid, go for it! No clear spaces? Hang a poster in your window!

2. Consider a theme or message you'd like to convey about Veterans Day, community service, bravery, unity, or other such themes.

3. Grab some chalk to trace your vision in place. Use chalk paint or a more permanent medium once you're sure of the design AND you own the place or have permission from an owner who understands your full intent and project scope.

4. Want some permanence or a bigger reach for your art? Take photos and post to your favorite socials.

Not feeling anything outdoor or large scale? Use the theme to create a postcard to send to a like-minded friend. Or just design digitally to post on your social media outlet(s).

## PROMPTS

### *Wonder – Write – What Next?*

Planning Area for Creative Messaging Activity
words | symbols | genre notes | materials list

1.



2.



3.

Sketch Your Favorite(s) Here:

Writing heals. If you're a veteran or know one, consider these opportunities to communicate experiences with peers, acquire author mentorship, and pursue publication:

**Veterans' Voices** enables military veterans to experience solace and satisfaction through writing with a program that envisions a world where people appreciate that writing can both heal and entertain. The program helps veterans process thoughts, feelings, and ideas they otherwise keep hidden, sometimes masking PTSD. By writing, many can build self-esteem and find healing.

**Veterans Writing Project** provides no-cost creative writing and songwriting workshops for veterans and their family members. It also publishes and produces work created by program participants. (www.VeteransWriting.org)

**The Veterans Writing Project** identifies emerging writers with U.S. military backgrounds and provides them with the tools and insights to nurture their passion for writing and navigating the entertainment industry. A program of The Writers Guild Foundation (www.WGFoundation.org)

List 3 people or programs that could benefit from these resources:

1.

2.

3.

# Light It Up

Hello, Neighbors!

Some say we should avoid telling kids about Santa Claus. Or at least stymie their belief shortly after toddlerhood. Well, bah humbug to that! The jolly man in red does more than bring the fa-la-la. Santa is all about happily sharing resources, community, and time. He embodies Nice over Naughty, Kind over Crass, and Generous over Grinch-y. All while accepting help from others with no expectation of reciprocity. Like Rudolph's nose, Santa's bright story can lead the way long after childhood. That's quite a lot from the jolly old seasonal wingman to the one who Christians worldwide call the Light of the World every day of the year.

Hanukkah, another seasonal mainstay for many, represents ideals we all can share, too. Springing from an important experience with a simple oil lamp, Hanukkah complements Santa's flare. Its eight nights have spread light and warmth for generations as the menorah's nine shining candles inspire recovery, dedication, and miracles from seemingly small things.

Many more fall-to-midwinter holidays celebrate the aspirational beauty and abiding power of light. If, like me, you miss summer's 9pm sunsets, then appreciating how people face the winter's early darkness is energizing.

- Diwali, a 2500-year-old Hindu-based festival of light, celebrates hope over despair and good over evil.

- Since 2009, Vivid Sydney in Australia has offered its annual 23-day display of illuminated art using eco-friendly LED lighting.

- The i Light Marina Bay Festival, makes Singapore shine, too.

- Kwanzaa's seven candles represent seven principals including unity, responsibility, creativity, and faith.

- The Jokkmokk Light Festival in Sweden's Lapland transforms the town with 3D projections on historic buildings and snow-covered landscapes.

- Thousands of Taiwan's Pingxi Lantern Festival participants write their wishes on paper sky lanterns then launched into open air.

- In Rio de Janeiro, they float a 280-foot Christmas tree decorated with three million lights on the Rodrigo de Freitas Lagoon.

- Loi Krathong, a lantern festival, gives thanks to sustaining waters by floating lights on bodies of water all over Thailand.

- America's largest nighttime parade, Chicago's annual Magnificent Mile Lights Festival, features 200+ lit trees and ends with great fireworks.

From Macao to Mexico and many places in between, people celebrate winter nights amid sparkling lights. Not to be outdone, the far-off stars shine quietly over each and every one of us.

Hooray for the many ways to ameliorate darkness! How and where will your light shine this month?

## PONDER & POST

This little light of mine, I'm gonna let it shine.
Public Domain

Darkness cannot drive out darkness; only light can do that.
Martin Luther King, Jr.

Living in the light of eternity changes your priorities.
Rick Warren

There is a crack in everything. That's how the light gets in.
Leonard Cohen

We realize the importance of light when we see darkness.
Malala Yousafzai

Light tomorrow with today!
Elizabeth Barrett Browning

There are two ways of spreading light: to be the candle or the mirror that reflects it.
Edith Wharton

## PRACTICAL | PROACTIVE | PRO-COMMUNITY

### Start Simple & Spread Out
*Shine On!*

Celebrate with light all year long! Enjoying a fireplace or candles at dinner are simple ways to add a glow to most any evening. Lanterns and subtle string lights are enhancing, too. Intentional lighting like Advent, Hanukkah, or birthday candles holds the busy-ness at bay.

Does your events calendar need more reasons to shine? Reconsider the list in the opening essay or do your own research to ways to glow up your days. Don't forget or make the underwhelming choice for the obvious dates, either. For example, 4th of July fireworks really are better live than on TV.

Share the aspirational symbolism of light with family and neighbors in simple ways:

1. Host a s'mores party. Ask everyone to bring their best, fanciest, or silliest light to the event. Know your crowd and specifically ban open torches and the like, as needed. Once gathered, offer prizes or just enjoy the glow.

2. Got a telescope or know a neighborhood stargazer? Invite others to gather under the stars somewhere with a clear view of the night sky. Get settled then turn off as much lighting as possible and look up. Ask your local expert to share fun facts. Or try free apps like Star Walk 2, Sky Tonight, and Stellarium Mobile.

3. Have you ever been 'Boo'ed' before Halloween? It's when kids 'sneak' to neighbors' front doors and tape paper ghost shapes that say 'Boo!' – just to get into the spirit. Borrow the pattern, but this time spread some light. Young ones can tape paper candles, flashlights, stars, or lanterns with messages like, "Shine on!" or "Be Sparkly!" or even one of the quotes offered above. If you link this to a light-centered holiday, add a "Happy Hanukah!" or similar to the design.

## Go Big & Go Home!

*Shining a Light on Not Shining Lights*

Metaphorically speaking, I hope that you always shine your own little light as well as reflect a thousand other points of light your community. However, non-metaphorically speaking, bright, shiny bulbs and fixtures are not always helpful. Often, the best option is to redirect, shield, or turn off physical lights.

Light pollution - the misuse or overuse of outdoor lighting – has serious impacts on ecosystems and human health. According to the National Park Service, "Light pollution can travel up to 200km away from its source." Happily, it also can be deterred with small but collective changes.

- Nearly half the species on Earth are nocturnal. Light pollution can affect vital ecological processes for wildlife. Minimize outdoor lights at night to protect navigation (bats), migration (birds), predator/prey interactions, reproduction, and habitat selection.

- Aim low. Pick fixtures with shades that keep light shielded to a small radius or aimed downward to help night fliers.

- Dark nights paired with bright days help stabilize our circadian rhythm which means quality sleep, a well-documented necessity for humans. After dark, use just enough light for safe navigation. Also, focus it very specifically just on tasks at hand.

- Both neighbors and nocturnal creatures hate blinding exterior lights. Use well-placed, movement-activated spots that provide just-in-time light for human safety and home security.

- Warm-white or amber color lighting is best for aesthetics and any fauna out after dark. Avoid blue blubs.

- Use a timer for landscape lighting; nobody wants glare coming in bedroom windows all night.

- Replace blown bulbs with efficient LEDs. They are energy-friendly and long-lived which saves on replacement costs.

- Adjust or replace outdoor lighting that beams with direct glare. Unnatural illumination diminishes dark vision, causing blind spots, and safety issues.

For detailed resources about lighting in your yard or on your street, see the Good Neighbor Toolkit at Utah State's 'Dark Skies Tool Kit' (https://extension.usu.edu/gnar/tools/ds-tools/dark-skies) You'll find some Citizen Science opportunities there, too.

Go darker! Gather some like-minded stargazers and apply for certification from The International DarkSky Places Program in the community, park, or urban place categories. DarkSky.org also offers many resources and helpful information to share with neighbors to create properly lit places for people and nature.

## PROMPTS

### *Wonder – Write – What Next?*

Which quote from the Ponder & Post section do you like best? Transcribe it here. Add sketches and doodles to enhance the message.

Translate the quote so toddler can understand it:

Transform the quote so it fits or replaces the lyrics or rhythm of a popular rap or hip-hop song with a 'light' theme:




Expand the quote so has one extra line that connects it to your favorite tradition, event, or holiday that is celebrated with light:




Draw and name a constellation that represents the light-infused holiday that your family likes to celebrate best.

# THANK YOU!

Hello, Neighbors!

Readers like you are a gift. Thank you for engaging with this book. I hope you found a sense of place – and a path to place making – in this, my heart-felt homage to community life.

This book is the result of feedback I received about the *Hello, Neighbors!* letters I wrote as the editor of my local community magazine. I still truly appreciate those early fans.

As residents, entrepreneurs, and service providers, my first readers frequently let me know that what I wrote about community cohesiveness was relevant and resonating. Here is some of my favorite input they shared:

> Our neighborhood magazine truly means a lot to our community, and we enjoy receiving it every month.
> 
> Aris M.

> I read all your letters; they're great. So interesting!
> 
> Happy Long-time Reader

Wow!!! What a wonderful writer.

Richie C

This magazine might be better than *Washingtonian Magazine*. It's not just the local insights, but the writing quality, too.

A Loyal Local Reader

What a lovely letter you wrote. It is certainly a nod to my belief that a higher consciousness will prevail. I have just returned from three weeks in India where 11,000 gathered from 139 countries and all religions to practice long synchronized meditation towards raising world consciousness. Smiles!

Karen

The writing is so good. It captures the spirit of our community.

A Fan

We're big fans. Personally, I always read everything from cover to cover. The magazine is a great asset to the community!

Sharon P

I read your whole 'Hello, Neighbors!' piece today. Enjoyed it very much. Your question at end - *How might your actions this month help you and others find love is all around?* - is a wonder-full way to be in our world.

...Hello, neighbors?! More attention to that question, please.

Mary S

Thus inspired, I wrote this book. I hope it keeps helping you recognize the best practices and the potential of the place where you come from. That it galvanizes you to develop the camaraderie and resources to infuse your household and neighborhood with increasingly meaningful connections.

If you have feedback to support this community of readers or questions about any of the ideas or resources shared in this book, please reach out to me via www.KatieEngen.com. Just saying, 'Hello!' would suit me fine, too.

www.ingramcontent.com/pod-product-compliance
Lightning Source LLC
Chambersburg PA
CBHW070526030426
42337CB00016B/2126